MW00624393

SEMIOTEXT(E) INTERVENTION SERIES

© Franco "Bifo" Berardi, 2018.

Published by Semiotext(e)
PO BOX 629, South Pasadena, CA 91031
www.semiotexte.com

Special thanks to Robert Dewhurst.

Inside cover photograph:
Design: Hedi El Kholti

ISBN: 978-1-63590-038-5
Distributed by The MIT Press, Cambridge, Mass.
and London, England
Printed in the United States of America

10 9 8 7 6 5 4 3 2

Franco "Bifo" Berardi

Breathing

Chaos and Poetry

semiotext(e)
intervention
series □ 26

Contents

Introduction

In 2011, in the wake of the Occupy movement, I published a small book titled *The Uprising: On Poetry and Finance*.[1] In that year, in many cities of the world large crowds of students, artists, and precarious workers gathered in the streets, occupied squares and public places, to call for an end to austerity measures and a restoration of democracies that had been obliterated by financial rule.

This moment was an illusion for many people, including me. Our sense of triumph, as you all remember, was illusory, to say the least. We did not stop financial plundering. We did not block, let alone reverse, one single measure of impoverishment, pillage, or devastation. In Egypt, the Occupy Tahrir movement launched a revolution and deposed the dictator Mubarak—only to see an Islamist win the subsequent election, and then a military coup seize power and install a new, possibly worse, dictator. Likewise, in other countries where Occupy had roused a few months of political participation, the techno-financial automatism of today's so-called governance soon imposed the rule of plunderers. Then, a sort of perfect storm struck the planet: local fragmentary wars spread all over, environmental devastation began to break out more and more often, and society grew poorer and poorer despite the increased output and bullish behavior of the stock market.

Should we conclude that Occupy was a failure? Yes and no. Yes, because it was unable to stop the neoliberal devastation and the fascist backlash that is now deploying worldwide as an incurable malady of the global mind. No, because Occupy was actually not—neither in its nature, in its internal dynamics, nor in the minds of many of its activists—a political attempt to seize power or to reverse existing power structures. Rather, Occupy was the beginning of a long-term process of reactivation of the social body, particularly that of the cognitive workers of the world. Only the self-organization of cognitive cyber-workers, only an alliance between the engineer and the poet, might reverse humanity's slide toward self-annihilation.

Seven years later, I come back to the subject that was at the center of *The Uprising*: the place of poetry in the relations between language, capital, and possibility. In *The Uprising*, I focused on poetry as an anticipation of the trend toward abstraction that led to the present form of financial capitalism. In this new book, I try to envision poetry as the excess of the field of signification, as the premonition of a possible harmony inscribed in the present chaos. Both in *The Uprising* and in *Breathing*, I call for a poetical reactivation of the erotic body of the general intellect as the only pathway of liberation from the oppression of financial capitalism. In *The Uprising*, this prospect was linked to a movement of physically occupying the public squares of the world, as a condition for the conjunction of political and physical bodies in urban space. In *Breathing*, I retrace the problem in terms of *respiration*: rhythm, spasm, suffocation, and death.

In 2011, the Occupy movement protested the submission of social life to semio-capital. As widespread as Occupy was, the movement was a political failure. Financial absolutism was not shaken by the protests, and indeed only hardened its grip, further destroying social life. Then impotence, humiliation, and despair led people to abandon any sentiment of humanist universalism and turn toward aggression and fascism; chaos invaded social life and the geopolitical map of the world. Dozens of Hitler imitators have now seized power everywhere as nationalism, racism, and religious fundamentalism have invaded public discourse.

But Occupy was not a political movement. The occupation of squares and public spaces was pointless, in political terms. Occupy, as I say, was the beginning of a long-term process aimed to the liberation of the social body from the abstract domination of financial absolutism, from the abstract grip that is suffocating social respiration just like airborne pollutants are spreading asthma and cancer to the lungs of the next generation.

In this new book, which is dedicated to our contemporary condition of breathlessness, I go back to the metaphor of poetry as the only line of escape from suffocation. Power is today based upon abstract relations between numerical entities. While the sphere of finance is ruled by algorithms that connect fractals of precarious labor, the sphere of life is invaded by flows of chaos that paralyze the social body and stifle breathing into suffocation. There is no political escape from this trap: only poetry, as the excess of semiotic exchange, can reactivate breathing. Only poetry will help us through the apocalypse that is already raging as an effect of decades of financial absolutism. Only poetry will soothe the suffering of the engineer's mind and the poet's mind, and will act to reverse the financial sphere's grip upon language.

The Uprising was an essay in the genealogy of financial power, from the point of view of language and particularly from the point of view of the "emancipation of signification from reality," which anticipated the emancipation of money from the real economy and a whole thread of abstraction that ran through the last century. *The Uprising* was a genealogical diagnosis.

Breathing is an essay on therapy. How do we deal with the suffocation that abstraction has produced in the history of humankind? Is there a way out from the corpse of financial capitalism?

inspiration

1

I CAN'T BREATHE

I suffer from asthma, so perhaps I was affected by a sense of asthmatic solidarity when I saw the video of Eric Garner's assassination. Garner was killed on July 17, 2014 in Staten Island, New York City, when a New York City Police Department officer put him in a chokehold for about fifteen to nineteen seconds while arresting him. The words "I can't breathe"—which Garner panted eight times, less and less audibly, before expiring—have been chanted by thousands of demonstrators all over the country in the months since.

In many ways, these words express the general sentiment of our times: physical and psychological breathlessness everywhere, in the megacities choked by pollution, in the precarious social condition of the majority of exploited workers, in the pervading fear of violence, war, and aggression. Trump is the perfect emperor for this baroque empire of unchained vulgarity, glamorous hypocrisy, and silent, widespread suffering.

Respiration is a subject that will help me discuss our contemporary chaos and search for an escape from the corpse of capitalism. I'll start by reading Friedrich Hölderlin.

Hölderlin belongs to the tradition of German Romanticism, but his pathway diverges from idealism because he opposes an ironic interrogation of Reality to the assertive style of Hegelian dialectic rationalism. Hegel chose the path of bigotry, the modern bigotry of History conceived as the becoming real of Truth.

Hölderlin was not such a bigot, and he did not follow this pathway that leads to historical delusion. In "Mnemosyne," he writes, "A sign we are, without interpretation / Without pain we are and have nearly / Lost our language in foreign lands."[1]

Hegel, who was a colleague of Hölderlin's during their college years in Tubingen, finds the unity of man in the concept, and in the historical "becoming true" of the concept. Hölderlin does not fall into the trapdoor of Hegel's *Aufhebung* (sublation). He does not buy idealism's faith in the historical realization of *Geist* (spirit). His ground for understanding reality is not *Geschichte* (History), but *Begeisterung* (inspiration). Hölderlin intuits that the intimate texture of being is breathing: poetical rhythm.

I intend to emphasize here the ontological meaning of "rhythm": foundationally, "rhythm" refers not only to vocal emissions or to the sound of acoustic matter, but also to the vibration of the world. Rhythm is the inmost vibration of the cosmos. And poetry is an attempt to tune into this cosmic vibration, this temporal vibration that is coming and coming and coming.

Mystical Buddhist philosophy distinguishes between the Indian words *shabda* and *mantra*. *Shabda* is a word for ordinary speech sounds, used to denote objects and concepts in the normal exchange of operational signifieds. A *mantra*, on the other hand, is a vocal sound that triggers the creation of mental images and sensible meanings. While *shabda* acts on the level of the operational chains of functional daily communication, *mantra* acts on the rhythm of the body and its relation with the semio-sphere—which is the source of the human world. *Ātman*, in this philosophy, is the singular breathing of each sensitive and conscious organism; *prana* is the cosmic vibration that we perceive as rhythm.

In "Notes on Antigone," Hölderlin opposes a poetical logic to the conceptual logic of the then-emerging idealism. Against Hegel's panlogism, Hölderlin advocates a sort of panpoeticism. We should not dismiss this stance as merely Romantic patheticism, for there is a deep philosophical core to

Hölderlin's suggestion. Hölderlin means that poetry is the semiotic flow that emanates the perceptual and narrative forms that shape the common sphere of experience. Reality, in other words, is the sphere of human interaction and communication secreted by language and refined by poetry. Poetry builds and instills the strata of mythopoiesis: it is the inspiration of the social imagination and of political discourse. In Hölderlin's words, "poets establish what remains."[2] Respiration and semiosis: this is the conceptual couple that I want to consider in order to understand something of our contemporary chaos.

Chaos and rhythm are the main threads of this book, which roams about the apocalypse of our time: in the second decade of the twenty-first century, the mindscape and the social scene are flooded by flows of unhappiness and violence. In his poetry, Hölderlin foresees the forthcoming chaos of modernity and the coming breathlessness. It's a problem of measure, he says. There is no earthly measure, so our sense of measure (rhythm) is only a projection of our breathing: poetry. This is why man lives poetically, although he "deserves" differently. Hölderlin: "May a man look up / From the utter hardship of his life / And say: Let me also be / Like these [gods]? Yes. As long as kindness lasts, / Pure, within his heart, he may gladly measure himself / Against the divine."[3]

Poetry as Excess

What is poetry? Why do human beings deal poetically with words, sounds, and visual signs? Why do we slip away from the level of conventional semiosis? Why do we loosen signs from their established framework of exchange?

Hölderlin writes, "Full of merit, yet poetically / Man dwells on this earth."[4] The poetical act is here opposed to the "deservingness," or merit, of man. What is merit? I think that merit is the quality of being worthy, of deserving praise or reward, the quality of measuring up to the (conventional) values of individuals in a given social scene.

Social beings are more or less full of merits. They deserve recognition as they exchange words and actions in a worthy way, and they receive mutual understanding as a sort of moral payment, a confirmation of their place in the theater of social exchange. Merits and moral payments and recognition are part of the conventional sphere. When humans exchange words in the social space, they presume that their words have established meanings and produce predictable effects. However, we are also able to utter words that break the established relation between signifier and signified, and open new possibilities of interpretation, new horizons of meaning.

In the last lines of the same poem, Hölderlin writes: "Is there measure on earth? There is /

None."[5] Measure is only a convention, an intersubjective agreement which is the condition of merit (social recognizability). Poetry is the excess which breaks the limit and escapes measure. The ambiguousness of poetical words, indeed, may be defined as semantic overinclusiveness. Like the schizo, the poet does not respect the conventional limits of the relation between the signifier and signified, and reveals the infinitude of the process of meaning-making (signification). Exactness and compliance are the conditions of merit and exchange. Excessiveness is the condition of revelation, of emancipation from established meaning and of the disclosure of an unseen horizon of signification: the possible.

What we are accustomed to call "the world" is an effect of a process of semiotic organization of prelinguistic matter. Language organizes time, space, and matter in such a way that they become recognizable to human consciousness. This process of semiotic emanation does not reveal a natural given; rather, it unfolds as a perpetual reshuffling of material contents, a continuous reframing of our environment. Poetry can be defined as the act of experimenting with the world by reshuffling semiotic patterns.

Did I say: poetry can be defined? Well actually the act of definition that I have just performed is arbitrary and illicit, because the question "What is poetry?" cannot be answered. I cannot say what poetry "is," because, actually, poetry "is" nothing. I can only try to say what poetry *does*.

The act of composing signs (visual, linguistic, musical, and so on) may disclose a space of meaning that is neither preexistent in nature nor based on a social convention. The poetical act is the emanation of a semiotic flow that sheds a light of nonconventional meaning on the existing world. The poetical act is a semiotic excess hinting beyond the limit of conventional meaning, and simultaneously it is a revelation of a possible sphere of experience not yet experienced (that is to say, the experienceable). It acts on the limit between the conscious and the unconscious in such a way that this limit is displaced and parts of the unconscious landscape—of what Freud called the "inner foreign country"—are illuminated (or distorted) and resignified.[6]

That said, I have so far said nothing, or nearly nothing. Very little. Actually, poetry is *the* act of language that cannot be defined, as "to define" means to limit, and poetry is precisely the excess that goes beyond the limits of language, which is to say beyond the limits of the world itself. Only a phenomenology of poetical events can give us a map of poetical possibilities.

"Is there measure on earth? There is / None," Hölderlin writes. He continues, "No created world ever hindered / The course of thunder."[7] Let's forget measure, let's forget technical capability social competence and functional proficiency. These measurable entities have invaded the modern mindscape and accelerated the rhythm of the info-sphere up to the point of the current psycho-collapse and techno-fascism. Let's try to think outside the sphere of measurability and of measure. Let's find a way to rhythmically evolve with the cosmos. Let's go out of this century of measure, let's go out to breathe together.

Félix Guattari speaks of "chaosmosis": the process of rebalancing the osmosis between the mind and chaos.[8] Hölderlin speaks of poetry as linguistic vibration, oscillation, and quest, of a rhythm tuned to the chaosmotic evolution that simultaneously involves mind and world.

VOICE SOUND NOISE

Chaos as Spasm

Chaosmosis is the title of Félix Guattari's final book.[1] The concept of chaosmosis emerged from Guattari's previous work, particularly from his and Gilles Deleuze's concept of the refrain (*ritournelle*). The term "chaosmosis" alludes to the incumbency of chaos, and the prospect of chaos's osmotic evolution itself. The groundwork of chaosmosis is the ceaseless interplay between cosmic respiration and refrains of singularity.

The established order—social, political, economic, and sexual—aims to enforce a concatenation that stiffens and stifles the vibrational oscillation of singularities. This stiffening of vibrant bodies results in what Guattari calls "spasms."[2] Guattari did not have time to further elaborate his concept of the chaosmic spasm, as he died a few months after the publication of *Chaosmosis*, but I think that this concept is crucial for an understanding of subjectivity under today's conditions of info-neural acceleration.

The spasm provokes suffering and breathlessness in the nervous system and the consciousness of the social organism. But the spasm is "chaosmic," in Guattari's terms, inasmuch as it invites the organism to remodulate its vibration and to create, ex nihilo, a harmonic order by way of resingularization. Music is the vibrational search for a possible conspiration beyond the limits of the noise of the environment, and the recomposition of fragments of noise in a sound that embodies a conscious vibrational intention. In the spasm sound collapses into noise, a tangle of inaudible voices.

Thinking with Guattari's chaosmosis, we may reframe the concepts of history and of historical time. When we speak of "history," when we view events from a historical perspective, we are imposing a certain modulation of our perception and projection of time. Historical perception is the effect of a mental organization of time within a teleological frame. Historical perception shapes time into an all-encompassing dimension that forces individuals and groups to share their temporalities according to a uniform meter and a teleological (or economic) frame. People enter the historical domain when they all hear more or less the same music in their ears. Time is captured by a certain rhythmic refrain, so people march at the same pace. This shared pace of time's temporality, perception, and projection is called "history." Only thanks to the harmonization of different temporalities can history frame time's myriad events within a common projectual narrative structure.

Time and Spasm

For Henri Bergson, time is defined from the point of view of our consciousness of duration. Time is the objectivation of a biological organism's act of breathing, which is sensitive and conscious. Singular respiration is concatenated with others' breathing, and this corespiration we name "society." Society is the dimension in which singular durations are rearranged in a shared time-frame.

Consciousness is located in time, but time is located in consciousness, as it can only be perceived and projected by consciousness. "Time" means the duration of the stream of consciousness, the projection of that dimension in which consciousness flows. The stream of consciousness, however, is not homogeneous: on the contrary, it is perceived and projected according to different rhythms and singular refrains, and sometimes it is codified and arranged into a regular, rhythmic repetition.

In the industrial age, when a dominant rhythm was imposed over the spontaneous rhythms of social subjects, power could be described as a code aligning different temporalities, an all-encompassing rhythm framing and entangling the singularity of individuals' refrains. We could speak of Political sovereignty when the sound of law was silencing the noise emitted from the social environment. In our contemporary connective postindustrial society, the opposite is true: power is no longer constructed by silencing the crowd (for example, through censorship, broadcast media, or the solemnity of political discourse), but is based on the boundless intensification of noise. Today, social signification is no longer a system of the exchange and decoding of signifiers, but a saturation of the listening mind—a neural hyperstimulation. While political order used to be effected by a voice proclaiming law amid the silence of the crowd, contemporary postpolitical power is a statistical function that emerges from the noise of the crowd.

Referring to the swarm-like behavior of networked culture, Byung-Chul Han summarizes the transformation that has occurred in the relation between power and information: "Shitstorms occur for many reasons. They arise in a culture where respect is lacking and indiscretion prevails. The shitstorm represents an authentic phenomenon of digital communication . . . *Sovereign is he who commands the shitstorms of the Net.*"[3] This is a good way to explain the ascent of the Emperor of Chaos to the highest political office in the world, the presidency of the United States of America. Modern power was based on the ability to forcibly impose one's own voice and to silence others: "Without the loudspeaker, we would never have conquered Germany," Hitler wrote in 1938 in the *Manual of German Radio.*[4] Now, power emerges from the storm of inaudible voices. Power no longer consists in eavesdropping and censoring. On the contrary, it stimulates expression and draws rules of control from the statistical elaboration of data emerging from the noise of the world. Social sound is turned into white noise and white noise becomes social order.

In Deleuze and Guattari's parlance, the "refrain" is a concatenation of signs, particularly phonetic sounds and phonetic vibrations; the refrain is a semiotic concatenation (*agencément sémiotique*) that enables the organism to enter its singular cosmos into a wider concatenation. Time is the projection of a singularity (*durée*, in Bergson) and is simultaneously the frame of interindividual conjunction, the grid where uncountable refrains interweave.

Music is a peculiar mode of chaosmosis: the osmotic process of transforming chaos into harmony. Music's process of signification is based on directly shaping the listener's body-mind: music is psychedelic (meaning, etymologically, "mind-manifesting").

Music deploys in time, yet the reverse is also true: making music is the act of projecting time, of interknitting perceptions in time. Rhythm is the mental elaboration of time, the common code that links time perception and time projection. The emanation of sound is part of the overall creation of a social cosmos: Steve Goodman speaks of "sonic warfare" in order to describe the invasion of society's acoustic sphere by sonic hypermachines that besiege acoustic attention, imposing a rhythm in which singularity is cancelled.[5]

Code, Debt, and the Future

Code is "speaking" us. Code is a tool for the submission of the future to language, enabled by the inscription of algorithms into the flux of language. The future is now being written by the algorithmic chain inscribed in techno-linguistic automatisms.

Prescriptions, prophecies, and injunctions are ways of inscribing the future in language, and, more pointedly, of actually producing the future by means of language. Like prescriptions, prophecies, and injunctions, code has the power to prescribe the future, by formatting linguistic relations and the pragmatic development of algorithmic signs. Financial code, for instance, triggers a series of linguistic automatisms which perform social activity, consumption patterns, and lifestyles.

"Money makes things happen. It is the source of action in the world and perhaps the only power we invest in," writes Robert J. Sordello in *Money and the Soul of the World.*[6] Money and language have something in common: they are nothing and yet affect everything. They are nothing but symbols, conventions, *flatus vocis*, yet they have the power to persuade human beings to act, to work, and to transform physical things. Language, like money, is nothing. Yet like money, language can do anything. Language and money are shaping our future in many ways. They are prophetic.

Prophecy is a form of prediction that acts on the development of the future by way of persuasion and emotion. Thanks to the social effects of psychological reactions to language, prophecy can be self-fulfilling. The financial economy, for instance, is marked by self-fulfilling prophecies. When ratings agencies downgrade the value of an enterprise or the value of a nation's economy, they make a prediction about the future performance of that enterprise or economy. But this prediction so heavily influences actors in the economic game that the downgrading results in an actual loss of reliability and an actual loss of economic value— thus fulfilling the prophecy. How can we escape the effects of prophecy? How can we escape the effects of code? These are two different problems, of course, but they share something in common.

Poetry as Semiotic Insolvency

In his preface to *Tractatus Logico-Philosophicus*, Wittgenstein writes, "in order to be able to draw a limit to thought, we should have to find both sides of the limit thinkable (i.e. we should have to be able to think what cannot be thought)."[7] Later, he posits:

> *The limits of my language* mean the limits of my world.
>
> Logic pervades the world: the limits of the world are also its limits.
>
> So we cannot say in logic, 'The world has this in it, and this, but not that.'
>
> [. . .]
>
> We cannot think what we cannot think; so what we cannot think we cannot *say* either.
>
> [. . .]
>
> The subject does not belong to the world: rather, it is a limit of the world.[8]

The potency and extension of language depend on the consistency of the subject: on its vision, on its situation. And the extension of my world depends on the potency of my language. The process of going beyond the limits of the world is what Guattari calls "chaosmosis." He speaks of chaosmosis "rekindling processes of semiotisation": i.e., redefining the semiotic grid.[9] The semiotic grid is a tangle that limits the possibilities of experience, and therefore limits the experienceable world itself.

"Chaosmosis" means breathing with chaos—"osmosis" implies breathing together—but in this osmosis with chaos a new harmony emerges, a new sympathy, a new syntony. This "emergence" is an effect of autopoietic morphogenesis: a new form emerges and takes shape when logical-linguistic conditions make it possible to see it and to name it. Only an act of language escaping the technical automatisms of financial capitalism will enable the emergence of a new life form. Only the reactivation of the body of the general intellect—the organic, existential, historical finitude that harbors the potency of the general intellect—will enable the imagination of new infinities.

Language has infinite potency, but the exercise of language happens in finite conditions of history and existence. Thanks to the establishment of a limit, the world comes to exist as a world of language. Grammar, logic, and ethics are all based on the imposition of a limit. Code is a limited exercise of language and, simultaneously, it is the imposition of a performing and productive limit. Limits can be productive, but outside of the space of limitation, infinite possibilities of language persist immeasurably.

Code implies syntactic exactness of linguistic signs: connection. Compatibility and consistency and syntactic exactness are the conditions of code's operational functionality. Code is language in debt. Only by exacting the necessary syntactic consistency can language perform its connective purpose. The leftover excess is the *remise en question* of language's infinity, the breakdown of consistency, the reopening of the horizon of possibility. Excess plays the game of conjunction (the game of bodies looking to make meaning out of *any* syntax), not the preformatted game of connection.

Poetry reopens the indefinite, through the ironic act of exceeding the established meaning of words. In every sphere of human activity, grammar establishes limits in order to define a space of communication. In the age of capitalism, the economy has taken the place of the universal grammar traversing the different levels of human activity: language, too, is defined and limited by its economic exchangeability. However, while social communication is a limited process, language is boundless: its potentiality is not limited by the limits of the signified. Poetry is the excess of language, the signifier disentangled from the limits of the signified. Irony, the ethical form of the excessive power of language, is the infinite game that words play to create and to skip and to shuffle meanings. Poetry and irony are tools for semiotic insolvency, for the disentanglement of language from the limits of symbolic debt.

CHAOS AND THE BAROQUE

The modern age blossomed with a breathtaking expansion of the sphere of experience: the discovery of the new world and the diffusion of printed texts paved the way for the expansion of experience and the enrichment of the imagination. This, in turn, led to the bewildering phantasmagoria called "the baroque." The humanist Renaissance of the fourteenth and fifteenth centuries had been founded on an assertion of the centrality of the human viewpoint in the vision of the landscape, in the projection of space, and in the construction of the world. The explosive Age of Discovery that followed multiplied prospective viewpoints.

In the sixteenth century, Spanish culture was the theater of a sort of vertiginous proliferation of viewpoints that José Antonio Maravall has called "baroque cosmovision."[1] Crowds of people coming from the countryside took hold of urban spaces, and the ensuing whirlwind of urban experience provoked an inflation of meaning and a sort of explosion of identity. In the same year that Columbus disembarked onto American soil, Spanish rulers ordered the expulsion of infidels. The country was just emerging from three centuries of religious war: religious identity, ethnic identity, and social identity now entered into the turmoil of modernity. The basic interrogation had to do with religious faith and ethnic belonging: in a word, with identity, a nonsense concept and a psychological trap. In the Spanish situation of the late fifteenth century, "Who are you?" was a twofold question. It meant, what is your origin? Are you a pure Christian or have your ancestors mingled with the infidels? Simultaneously it meant, what social place do you have?

The problematics and the adventures of the picaresque novel (that literary genre that was emerging from the urban condition and from the conflict between the bourgeoisie and urban proletarians) are grounded here. A *picaro* is someone who has nothing: no property, no job, not even the certainty of his origin. Therefore, the *picaro* is someone who is searching. The *picaro*, in fact, is a *buscòn*, a searcher. What is the *picaro* searching for? He is searching for everything, and first of all for himself—for his origin, his identity. The bewilderment that Góngora calls "madness" (*locura*) and

Quevedo perceives as "disillusion" (*desengano*) was an effect of this deterritorialization of viewpoints and proliferation of stimuli. The baroque is a transition, according to Deleuze. A transition from what to what? A gigantic fluctuation happened in the European semio-sphere when, thanks to the technology of print, written text spread among a large urban population, while geographic explorations enormously expanded the limits of the known world. This fluctuation led the collective mind to peer beyond the borders of the anthropocentric order asserted by Renaissance culture. That order was scrambled by the man-made disorder of baroque modernity: artifice replaced nature, *locura* replaced reason, and appearance replaced being. Lost in the urban labyrinth, in the unremitting battle for survival and accumulation, reason turned into shrewdness and measure was replaced by force. The *buscòn*—the searcher—became the symbol of the new condition.

The fold, the fractal: these are the figures of the baroque imagination. The baroque originated from a vertiginous fractalization of the humanist order. For the first time, inflation appeared as an economic and a semiotic phenomenon. Catapulted to a planetary dimension, the Spanish economy was shaken by social turmoil and by inflation, while the Spanish psycho-sphere was frenzied with a proliferation of signs: inflation of meaning, *locura.* Economic inflation happens when more and more money is needed to buy fewer and fewer goods, and semiotic inflation happens when more and more signs buy less and less meaning. Chaos loomed in the frantic acceleration of the info-sphere during the Spanish Golden Age, and it is in this conjuncture that the baroque imagination is rooted.

Then, in the age of scientific revolution, of industrialization and of nation-states, bourgeois rationalism prevailed, and the baroque sensibility retreated to linger around the margins of modern art and philosophy. But at the end of modernity rationalism faded, and in the twilight of humanism that we are living through today, a new gigantic fluctuation is perceptible. Reason has been submitted to financial rule, such that the culture of belonging has replaced universal reason and identitarian resentment has replaced social solidarity. The legacies of humanism and the Enlightenment are nullified along with the legacy of socialism. Socialism, however, has returned under the shape of national socialism: the discourse and the political agenda of Trump, Putin, Salvini, Erdogan, and Modi. The promise of recovering the economic security destroyed by neoliberal globalism is tied to the promise of empowering the nation (the identitarian particularity) against those who do not belong.

In the folds of the contractual sensibility that results from the digital kingdom of abstraction and from the aggressive return of identity, we are baroquely searching for a new rhythm.

Indeterminacy and Chaos

In the wake of Newton and Galileo, modern mechanistic physics was based on the idea of a unifying language—the language of mathematics—which was supposed to be apt to semiotize the whole of creation. Later on, the development of biology and biogenetics thrived on the assumption of a deterministic code that ruled the organism's development. In the 1950s, a fusion of physics and biology led to the discovery of DNA. The body was then viewed as a deployment and actualization of code, of an implied order which accounted for the unfolding of life. This mechanical vision of nature coincided with an economic practice based on the measurability of all things: labor time as the source of economic value, and value measured as a product of working time. In industrial society, the determinability of economic value was based on the fact that labor time was definable as an average term. One could determine the economic value of an object by calculating the time which was socially necessary in order to produce it.

But at the end of modern industrialism, the deterministic relationship between labor, time, and value is now dissolving in the chaotic dimension of semio-capitalism. When the measurability of value dissolves, when time becomes aleatory and singular, the very idea of determination starts to fade. This affects the realm of the natural sciences too, where the discourse of determinism is abandoned and replaced by the principle of indeterminacy.

In the nineteenth century, Pierre-Simon de Laplace envisioned a universal intelligence able to know every state and every possible evolution of beings:

> An intelligence that, at a given instant, could comprehend all the forces by which nature is animated and the respective situation of the beings that make it up, if moreover it were vast enough to submit these data to analysis, would encompass in the same formula the movements of the greatest bodies of the universe and those of the lightest atoms. For such an intelligence nothing would be uncertain, and the future, like the past, would be open to its eyes. The human mind affords, in the perfection that it has been able to give to astronomy, a feeble likeness of this intelligence.[2]

This universal intelligence would be able to encompass with a single formula the movements of the largest bodies and the movements of the slightest atoms, and therefore, as a consequence of ruling out any uncertainty, it would be able to foretell the future. This intelligence would be determinist in a double sense: it would be the cause of the inmost determination and simultaneously it would be the consciousness presiding over any deterministic relationship occurring in nature.

But Laplace's deterministic rationalism did not survive the unfolding of a new epistemology: the concept of chaos entered into the scientific realm when the progressive order of modernity started to crumble and when the destabilizing force of the financial market started to jeopardize the economic order of industrialism. The concept of indeterminacy obliged to rethink the relation between the mind and world in terms of undecidability, and at this point chaos entered the fray.

In science, just as in life, sometimes a sequence of events may reach such a level of complexity that a small perturbation will have huge, unpredictable effects. We speak of "chaos" when such indeterminacy becomes widespread. "Chaos" stands for an environment that is too complex to be decoded by our available explanatory frames, an environment in which fluxes circulate too quickly for our minds to elaborate. The notion of chaos denotes a complexity which is too dense and too fast for our brains to decipher. Chaos takes a special place today in the sphere of the social sciences, as the order of modern civilization is falling apart.

Modern civilization may be described as a process of the colonization of reality by the force of the law, in a double sense. Scientific law wanted to reduce the becoming of physical matter to the repetition of a model, while political law was a linguistic act that asserted a conventional norm and then aimed to oblige social activity to conform to it. The subjugation of natural chaos by the humanistic order of measurement (recall that "ratio," in Latin, means measure) was the crucial feature of the cultural colonization of the world by the Europeans. Civilization was—or better, was conceived as—the transformation of Chaos into Order. That transformation implied an act of matemathizing the world that enabled a commen-surabilization (a proportioning and submittal to measurement). Scientific knowledge implies a limitation of the space of what is relevant, an exci-sion of the irrelevant. Similarly, the political mind cannot be decisive without delimiting the space of what is socially relevant. Only what is relevant from the viewpoints of knowledge and govern-ment is actually elaborated by the modern mind. Forget the irrational, forget mythology, forget craziness and delirium. Those multiple facets will be segregated in the madhouse that psychiatry is building in order to protect the Enlightenment from the darkness.

Machiavelli distinguished the sphere of Fortune (*fortuna*) from the sphere of Will (*volere*). The prince is the (male) person who subdues Fortune (chance, which is feminine) to the masculine will—to measure, to order and predictability. Fortune is the chaos that is always hiding in the folds of the human mind, and if the Prince wants to govern, he has to preemptively carve a narrow chain of events from the infinite territory of Fortune. The dark infinity of unreducible chaos lies at the border of the established order. Rhythm is the key that enables the synchronization between Fortune and Will, between reality and reason. But only a tiny part of the sphere of reality can be synchronized with reason, and only a tiny part of Fortune can be synchronized with political will. This tiny part is what is called "relevant" by the ruling intellect of Order. Government is always an illusion, as political consciousness carves out a tiny chain of relevant social events and tries to protect this space—the space of civilization—from the surrounding ocean of ungovernable matter.

The digital intensification of the semiotic flow has broken the rhythm that we have inherited from the modern age. When the refrain of rationalism and political reason grows unable to process and govern the flows of information proliferating in the networked info-sphere, the protective fence of relevancy breaks down, and we can no longer distinguish what is relevant from what is not. If cyberspace is the virtual intersection of infinite mental stimuli, and cybertime is the mental rhythm of processing these stimuli, how can cybertime be upgraded to the point of processing today's digital cyberspace? As far as I know, we cannot speed up our mental rhythm beyond a certain limit that is physical, emotional, and cultural.

When the acceleration of cyberspace breaks the rhythm of mental time, and we no longer know what is relevant and what is irrelevant in our surrounding environment, this is what we call "chaos": the inability to attribute meaning to the flow, the breakdown of our framework of relevance. A special vibration of the soul spreads out at this point, which we call "panic": the subjective recording of chaos.

4

CHAOS AND THE BRAIN

> Here all is distance;
> there it was breath.
> —Rainer Maria Rilke, "The Eighth Elegy"

The Apocalyptic Unconscious

Social psychomancy is not a science, it's just a game that I play from time to time in order to survey the ongoing history of humankind from the viewpoint of the social unconscious. So do not take me too seriously. Social psychomancy is a random methodology for the interpretation of a random sphere of events: mental events evoked by the flows of imagination that roam the social psychosphere and are organized by forces of attraction and repulsion. Fears, expectations, desires, and resentments dwell in the psychomantic sphere of imagination, so I think of psychomancy as the art of mapping the collective mind. The history of the world cannot be fully grasped if we do not understand what happens in the social psycho-sphere: shared meaning, rational goals, and conscious motivations are continuously disrupted and reshaped by the immaterial substances that social psychomancy tries to survey.

The present may be considered the Age of the Dark Enlightenment: the age of the rejection of modernity's rationalistic Enlightenment by those who have been led to submit reason and life to the ferocity of financial mathematics. Rational categories have lost their grasp on our social becoming, and we need a different approach in order to apprehend our contemporary postrational condition. Our time is traversed by an apocalyptic sentiment of a sort. The institution most credited for interpreting the famous text ascribed to John of Patmos— the Catholic Church, whose expertise is long established—has lately been shaken by astounding, unheard-of events.

In 2005 Karol Wojtyla, the pope who triumphed in the long fight against the Soviet Union's Empire of Evil, performed a worldwide broadcasted spectacle of extreme physical suffering and fortitude. After his death, a new pope, of German origin, came to Rome proclaiming the unquestionable uniqueness of Truth and condemning relativism. Then, on a dark night in February 2013, while the black sky of Rome was ripped by lightning, Pope Benedict bent his head and acknowledged his own fragility and the fragility of the human mind. Chaos was spreading around the world, and the word of Truth was imperceptible amidst the fury and fog of the uncountable wars that were destroying the lives of people all over the planet.

At that point, the Holy Spirit chose a new pope, an Argentinean who introduced himself to a crowd of the faithful with the words "Good evening, I am a man who comes from the end of the world." What he meant was "I come from a country where people like me have experienced the apocalypse provoked by financial capitalism." He was the first pope in church history to name himself Francis: a defiant declaration of affinity with the poor, with the exploited, with those who have been oppressed by the economic powers of the world. This defiance was not unconnected to a daring rethinking of theological grounding. In the first interview that Pope Francis released, to Monsignor Santoro for the magazine *Civiltà Cattolica* in October 2013, he spoke of theological virtues, inviting Christians to emphasize charity rather than faith and hope. The church, he said, is like a military hospital in wartime: our mission is not to judge nor convert, but to heal the wounds of human persons regardless of their religious faith, ethnic origin, or nationality.[1] A glimpse of internationalism shone in his words, and in subsequent years Francis has emerged as the main actor of human resistance and dignity in an age of spreading barbarity.

Beyond the political meaning of his actions, I think that Francis is speaking to the apocalyptic unconscious of our time, while trying to translate this into an ethical soteriology, or soteriological ethics. Only in the embrace of the other, only in social solidarity, can we find any shelter. God's silence resounds in the background, and in different ways the contemporary artistic sensibility is speaking the same language. Nanni Moretti (in *Habemus Papam*), Martin Scorsese (in the not so convincing *Silence*), and Paolo Sorrentino (in the enigmatic *The Young Pope*) in different ways elaborate on the same subject. The silence of God resounds as chaos, as we have grown unable to breathe at the rhythm of our own respiration, which has been captured by the apocalyptic force of the algorithm of financial capitalism.

Chaos and Concepts

In the last chapter of *What Is Philosophy?*, Deleuze and Guattari reflect on aging. They refer to senescence in terms of the relation between order and chaos:

We require just a little order to protect us from chaos. Nothing is more distressing than a thought that escapes itself, than ideas that fly off, that disappear hardly formed, already eroded by forgetfulness or precipitated into others that we no longer master. These are infinite *variabilities*, the appearing and disappearing of which coincide. They are infinite speeds that blend into the immobility of the colorless and silent nothingness they traverse, without nature or thought. This is the instant of which we do not know whether it is too long or too short for time. We receive sudden jolts that beat like arteries. We constantly lose our ideas. That is why we want to hang on to fixed opinions so much. We ask only that our ideas are linked together according to a minimum of constant rules.[2]

"Chaos" is defined here in terms of speed, of acceleration of the info-sphere relative to the slow rhythms of reason and of the emotional mind. When things start to flow so fast that the human brain grows unable to elaborate the meaning of information, we enter into the condition of chaos.

What has to be done in such a situation? My suggestion is that you should not focus on the flow, but on your breath. Don't follow the external rhythm, but breathe normally. Deleuze and

Guattari: "the *struggle against chaos* does not take place without an affinity with the enemy, because another struggle develops and takes on more importance—the struggle *against opinion*, which claims to protect us from chaos itself."[3] Those who wage war against chaos will be defeated, as chaos feeds on war. When chaos is swallowing the mind (including the social mind), we should not be afraid of it, we should not strive to subjugate chaos to order. That will not work, because chaos is stronger than order. So, we should make friends with chaos, and in the whirlwind we should look for the superior order that chaos brings in itself.

In the same place, Deleuze and Guattari describe the relation of poetry to such chaos: "In a violently poetic text, Lawrence describes what produces poetry: people are constantly putting up an umbrella that shelters them and on the underside of which they draw a firmament and write their conventions and opinions. But poets, artists, make a slit in the umbrella, they tear open the firmament itself, to let in a bit of free and windy chaos and to frame in a sudden light a vision."[4] Reading these lines, I cannot help but recall Wittgenstein's famous sentence in the *Tractatus*: "*The limits of my language* mean the limits of my world."[5] People are constantly sheltering themselves under the umbrellas of their limited languages, and their worlds are written on the undersides of these umbrellas. Poets cut the fabric of the umbrella and their incision discloses the unbearable vision of the true firmament. The poet's action is literally apocalyptic, and it begins the unchaining (or disentanglement) of the hidden possibilities lying there since the beginning, since the cosmic primeval origins of human history.

Poetry opens multiple ambiguous pathways to meaning, and concepts act in a similar way. Concepts are created to frame our cognition: a concept, etymologically speaking, is a captor of different entities, material and purely intellectual ("concept" comes from the Latin *concipere*, which literally means "taking together"). As Deleuze and Guattari write, "A concept is therefore a chaoid state par excellence; it refers back to a chaos rendered consistent, become Thought, mental chaosmos. And what would *thinking* be if it did not constantly confront chaos? Reason shows us its true face only when it 'thunders in its crater.'"[6]

The cosmos is the background of the process of recomposition that happens at the existential and at the historical level. "Cosmos," in fact, means order and simultaneously the all-encompassing dimension that exceeds human history and individual existence. Chaosmosis is the opening of the ordered system to chaotic flows and the osmotic vibration of the organism that looks for a rhythm tuned to the cosmos. I consider *Chaosmosis* and *What Is*

Philosophy? to be the books that philosophically predict the new millennium: philosophy now has to posit itself on the threshold of chaos without fearing the swirl, and without worshipping its vertigo and surrendering to its fascination.

In *What Is Philosophy?*, the two old boys speak of a struggle against chaos, but they also suggest that chaos may be a friend, a new condition of thought. The modern order wanted to protect us against chaos. We have accepted that deal, and we have implicitly accepted an order based on exploitation and misery. In order to avoid being killed by hunger or by barbarians, we have accepted the salaried labor and the daily war of competition. But now that the order based on salaried labor order is crumbling and the universal framework of modern rationality is dissolving, the protectors are turning into predators. So order turns into chaos, but in the chaos we should detect the outlines of an implicit new harmony for the challenge we now face is this: we must make visible an order where now we see only incomprehensible darkness. The word "order," actually, is misleading: we are not speaking of order, we are in fact speaking of rhythm. A new rhythm is what humankind needs.

Chaos has the potency to make creation possible. Can the collective brain consciously master and attune to the evolution of the collective brain itself?

Chaos and Aging

"We require just a little order to protect us from chaos," Deleuze and Guattari write.[7] The aging philosophers wanted to be protected. Protected from what? From the chaotic features of the world? I don't think so. They didn't want protection from the chaotic world, but from the brain's chaos.

The aging brain is an agent of chaos, because the brain grows slower and less precise. Neuronal geometry loses its definition and projects this loss of definition onto the surrounding world. In the senescent decay of the psycho-sphere we can find an explanation of the current explosion of chaos. The average age of the human brain is growing older, while the amount of nervous info-stimuli is exploding. In past centuries, senility was such a rare experience that the old person was automatically considered a wise man (or an idiot). But now the pyramid of age is almost squared, and old people are so common that it's getting more and more difficult to care for them, and to tend to the expanding sphere of dementia, memory loss, Alzheimer disease, and . . . chaos. Aging is a distinctive mark of the postmodern era: loss of energy, loss of speed, mental confusion.

Chaos is essentially a problem of tempo. When we call it "chaos," we mean that our surrounding environment (particularly the information that invades our attention sphere) is too fast to decipher, too fast for us to possibly decode and remember. History can no longer be understood in terms of a narrative, and instead takes the shape of a semiotic hurricane, an unchaining of uninterpretable flows of neurostimuli. No one has better expressed the sentiment of being overwhelmed by chaos than Shakespeare:

> Out, out, brief candle,
> Life's but a walking shadow, a poor player
> That struts and frets his hour upon the stage
> And then is heard no more. It is a tale
> Told by an idiot, full of sound and fury,
> Signifying nothing.[8]

Chaos implies sound and fury, but it also implies a special relation with signification.

While globalization has linked the daily lives and activities of all people living on the planet, the imagination of the planet's masses is less and less retraceable to a common frame of historical narration. In a paradoxical reversal, economic globalization has broken the universality of reason and the political sentiment of internationalism: nationalism, racism, and religious fundamentalism are the cultural identity markers claimed by the globalized masses of the world. So history turns into idiocy, a tale told by an idiot.

But we should see the other side of this idiotization of history: Might this idiot be trying to speak of something that is untranslatable into our known language? Might the idiot be saying something that exceeds our understanding, because his noise and his fury require a different system of interpretation, a different language, a different rhythm? Certainly now, in the second decade of the first century of the third millennium, the human brain as a whole and all the individual brains of humans seem to be overwhelmed by the accelerating pace of the surrounding universe: the human brain has become outpaced by the rhythm of its surrounding environment. When we say "chaos," then, we mean two different, complimentary movements. We refer to the swirling of our surrounding semiotic flows, which we receive as if they were "sound and fury." But we also refer to attempts to reconcile this encompassing environmental rhythm with our own intimate, internal rhythm of interpretation.

conspiration

5

CHAOS AND CONTROL

Modern Panlogical Projects

Modernity is overshadowed by two panlogical projects, one envisioned by Leibniz and the other by Hegel. The Hegelian logos is embodied in the tragedy of history: reason in Hegel astutely asserts itself through the bloody and tortuous events that turn the daily life of the people into History (*Geschichte*). Hegel's panlogical project provides a conceptual map of the road to our present reality marked by unremitting violence. The drive toward totalization—the horizon of the Hegelian *Aufhebung*—has generated the wreckage whose effects we are witnessing now, in the age of Trump, the age of dementia fuelled by the full realization of reason in its techno-financial form. As the failure of this historical panlogism is today certified by the explosion of widespread dementia and global civil war, a second panlogical project is emerging, as algid and glimmering as a castle of ice: the project of computational recombination that is the legacy of Leibniz.

According to Leibniz, reason deploys in an abstract sphere where bodies are not allowed. Nevertheless, bodies are now dwelling in a world that is ruled by computation. Computational theology has subsumed social life and language, generating a cascade of determination. In this space of determination, bodies can act effectively only if they are compatible with the format of the reigning mathematical theology; otherwise, they are marginalized as irreducible residuals. Leibnizian computational panlogic is a logic of simultaneous generation and control. This logic does not deal with the physical and historical reality of bodies, but with the virtual condition of computational monads, to which real bodies are obliged to conform.

Let's look at the landscape of this postdialectical century: while historical bodies are decaying and exploding in the chaotic sphere of global civil war, forever dissipating the prospect of progress and *Aufhebung*, in the virtual bunker a Leibnizian ur-monad is generating connective concatenation as a continuous flux of disembodied recombination. Leibniz's monad is the zero-dimensional generative potency of information. The very expression "incorporeal automata" descends from Leibniz's imagination. In the *Monadology*, he uses this phrase to refer to the mathematical generation of entities: "One could give the name *entelechies* to all simple substances or created monads. For they all have in them a certain perfection (*echousi to enteles*); there is a certain self-sufficiency (*autarkeia*) that makes them sources of their own internal actions and, so to speak, incorporeal automata."[1]

In his short essay titled "Principles of Nature and Grace, Based on Reason," Leibniz writes that "each living mirror that represents the universe according to its own point of view, that is, each *monad*, each substantial center, must have its perceptions and its appetites as well ordered as is compatible with all the rest."[2] Leibniz refers to a principle of algorithmic regulation proceeding from the all-generating computer named God, traversing the whole universe and informing each fragment according to a recombinant methodology. This generative panlogism, perfectly epitomized by the all-encompassing digital principle of recombination, does not recognize the suffering of pulsating living bodies, does not perceive the chaotic violence of exploitation, corruption, and war, but only recognizes the flow of data that gives artificial life and syntactic exchangeability to the informational units that are working, producing value, and interacting in the space of the theological economy. As he writes in the *Monadology*, "each organic body of a living being is a kind of divine machine or natural automaton which infinitely surpasses all artificial automata."[3] God is here the binary principle of generation that emanates perfectly compatible units in recombination. As he writes, "God alone is the primary unity or the original simple substance, of which all the created or derivative monads are products."[4] This panlogical vision of the world—that perfectly prefigures the late modern dynamics of digital combinatory concatenation and financial capitalism—is based on the Leibnizian conception of language as *caracteristica universalis*, an artificial language that should act as the principle of a purely rational grammar.

Hegel's own panlogism is based on a methodology of disjunction and overcoming (*Aufhebung*), and it interprets the mode of conjunction dialectically: Truth is revealed at the end of the historical process as an effect of conflict and recomposition. Language penetrates the historical dimension and is penetrated by historical dynamics. When modernity's promise collapses, when chaos replaces the project of reason and war replaces the political order, we leave these spheres of conjunctive concatenation and historical realization. At this point, we say goodbye to Mr. Hegel and enter the sphere of computation, in which reason is not the endpoint of the historical process, a *telos* pursued by the conscious action of men, but is its beginning, the generative source of countless recombinations. Digital reason replaces historical reason, and the spiritual necessity of historic realization (*Aufhebung*) is replaced by the mathematical necessity of a logical machine that entangles human language and living events.

Chaos and Control

In *Technics and Civilization*, Lewis Mumford compares the world dominated by machines to the Greek Hades, the land of the dead populated by ghosts, the realm of shadows. Here we are.

In the last five decades, the anthropo-sphere has undergone a mutation based on the evolution of language, and particularly an evolution of the techno-semiotic concatenation. We have taken part in the creation of a digital network and in the proliferation of cellular smartphone connections that enormously intensify the density and the invasiveness of neuro-info stimuli.

This interactive grid has pervaded daily life and is slowly reformatting cognitive activity in the sense of an increasing compliance between mind and the digital network. The diffusion of immersive virtual environments, accessible thanks to portable gadgets for 3D synaesthetic immersion, is about to expand our dependence on simulated environments. And the construction of AI systems and cognitive self-learning machines is intended to perfect the process of android creation. These technological steps are paving the way to the Ultimate Automaton, the Leibnizian recombinant panlogical machine. A question looms, however: Will the tendency toward the Ultimate Automaton be compatible with the embodied evolution of organic brains? Will the self-learning synthetic android assimilate and fully dominate the sphere of language and communication? The answer cannot be merely technical, because the evolution of linguistic machines interacts with the evolution (perhaps, the involution) of conscious and sensitive organisms whose reflexes are not technically determinable.

Abstraction has been recently gaining ground. The financialization of the economy is the most evident proof of this expansion of the realm of abstraction. But the increasing subjugation of life to abstraction is now provoking a backlash: life is reacting to abstraction, and this return of vitality has taken the shape of an aggressive reaffirmation of identity—national, religious, racial. The return of the body—the brainless body that has been detached from universal reason and from bodily compassion—is resulting in the emergence of postmodern fascism worldwide. Here, two trends are technologically intertwined and are culturally diverging: the first is based on the innervation of the digital network in the neural system and the ensuing hyperconnection of the brain; the second is based on the demented explosion of the body detached from the disembodied brain. This explosion manifests itself in the identitarian frenzy which is now devastating the political order of human civilization. Having lost any faith in the universality of reason, having no access to the sphere of decision making, people cling to imaginary identities based on the mythologies of nation, race, and religion.

So the abstract order of the control systems coexists and interweaves with the chaos of the hyperstimulated mind of the global metropolis. The expanding sphere of automation and control might be leading toward the submission of social life to a neuro-totalitarian form of order. In the contemporary simmering magma of political and mental chaos, technology appears as a separate sphere of perfect order, and this order gives consistency and continuity to the fragmentary events of the daily business of life, even as consciousness and political will grow unable to deal with hypercomplex automation. The two spheres, living chaos and technological order, are diverging, but they feed each other.

What will happen in the long run? Will the destructive force of the brainless body tear human civilization apart, and plunge the world into an abyss of nuclear devastation or hellish pollution and permanent war? Will, instead, the abstract potency of the disembodied brain overcome the identitarian madness and submit the individual brains of each inhabitant of our planet to the all-pervading force of the Ultimate Automaton?

I rather expect that the two trends will coexist and interact. Human civilisation seems poised to evolve in a disjointed way: civilization is going to survive, but it is going to be no longer human. Humankind will survive, but will be less and less civilized—unless we find a new tuning between the emotional mind and the neuro-machine.

Neuro-totalitarianism

As far as I know, no political thinker of the last fifty years has been able to imagine a future scenario resembling our present with the perspicuity of Philip K. Dick, who described the coevolution of synthetic organisms and decaying urban environments. From his works we receive the imagination of an intermingling continuum of rotting *bios* and computational machines.

Today, technology is hostage to war and war is hostage to technology. Neuro-totalitarian tendencies are actually at work in the interaction between human cognition and networked automata, yet the overall transformation is not leading to a condition of political order. Rather, the reverse is happening, because the organic and neurological substance that society is made of is finally exceeding technological control. Technology penetrates the organic body and shapes its cognitive activity, but the body ceaselessly secretes unassimilable substances: the excesses of life, of Eros, of the unconscious. These excesses are generating disruptions and breakdowns. The more pervasive technological control, the more disruptions tend to spread. The more social life depends on techno-control and automation, the more disruptions may provoke catastrophic effects. Indeterminacy is inherent to the bio-social sphere, while techno-automation is based on mathematical determinism. A small amount of indeterminacy may lead to enormous amounts of disruption. As automated systems are more and more interconnected, disruptions tend to spread and proliferate. This is why I suggest that the automated world is simultaneously a space of order and chaos—order in the sphere of connection, and chaos in the interaction of the connected sphere with the pulsating sphere of conjunctive bodies.

We're used to believing that machines are built, while human beings grow, that machines only move as directed, while human beings move autonomously. These assumptions no longer correspond to reality. Human beings are moving less and less autonomously, and relying more and more on technical prostheses, while machines are learning to learn and becoming endowed with powers of self-replication.

What happens when machines grow able to direct themselves, to repair themselves, to teach themselves? What happens when machines impose their order on the chaos of the brain?

The project Neuralink aims to create brain-computer interfaces. The direct electro-stimulation of synaptic chains has long been envisioned in science-fiction literature. In the medical realm, electrode arrays and other implants have been used to help ameliorate the effects of Parkinson's, epilepsy, and other neurodegenerative diseases. In 2017, Tesla CEO Elon Musk spoke about human fate in clearly techno-determinist terms, arguing that we have to turn ourselves into cyborgs if we wish to survive the rise of artificial intelligence. "Over time I think we will probably see a closer merger of biological intelligence and digital intelligence. It's mostly about the bandwidth, the speed of the connection between your brain and the digital version of yourself," he commented.[5]

From Flyover to Immersion

The current production of virtual reality interfaces will likely pervade the psycho-sphere of a large part of humanity, inasmuch as the real world is getting so distressing that those who will be able to do so will transmigrate into a more tolerable universe. As Web 2.0 enabled access to a boundless info-sphere of social interaction, Web 3.0 will likely offer access to an archive of fully simulated experiences: synaesthesis, immersion in perceptual universes.

Twenty-five years of the increasing pervasiveness of the digital network have produced a mutation in the format of enunciation-reception-interpretation among conscious and sensitive organisms. The connective rationale has penetrated and reshaped the semiotic line of exchange up to the point of making social molecules unable to conjoin, unable to access the sensuous realm of conjunction. A new phase of this digital mutation emerges: the sensorium itself plunging into computational environments of simulated experience. Synthetic life.

Web 2.0 has allowed for a condition of continuous flyover: the subject cannot fully experience the entire field of information and exchange, and is flying over it in such a way that the closer it gets, the more the field enlarges and escapes. The acceleration of the informational cycle enabled by broadband has produced an effect of continuous chasing: the user is only a spectator to a flow that goes faster and faster, so he is always feeling late, caught in an endless chase after the elusive flurry of information. Broadband and the high-speed Web put us in a persistent condition of being out of sync. The imminent immersive net of Web 3.0, on the contrary, may halt the acceleration and oblige the user to return to the present, if it is a replicable present generated by software: a simulation of life that must be experienced in real time, immersively.

Having been thrown into an environment of purely functional impulses, the agent of language has undergone a sensorial deprivation, a psychical impoverishment of affective reflexes. Grown in a digital environment, accustomed to react to discrete, quantifiable changes of state, the individual tends to lose its sensitivity to existential nuances and to the ambiguity of conjunctive communication. The immersive Web is intended to facilitate synaesthetic experiences and to enable the sharing of perceptual environments and the projection of synthetic universes. Consequently, access to the immersive Web of shared simulated experiences will undermine the concept of experience as the singular adventure of an organism that perceives and projects. A philosophical question will arise: Can we experience experience? Can we live a life that we are unable to live or even to imagine, but that has been imagined for us by computer engineers and life designers?

6

PURITY

the terrors of technocracy, which sought to liberate humanity from its humanness through the efficiency of markets and the rationality of machines. This was the truly eternal fixture of illegitimate revolution, this impatience with irrationality, this wish to be clean of it once and for all.

—Jonathan Franzen, *Purity*

Epidemics

I spent the first years of the eighties in Manhattan. It was the most exciting of times. I went there as a writer for a music magazine based in Milan. I was writing about New York's postpunk No Wave scene, and about street art, Keith Haring's graffiti, and Rammellzee and Basquiat.

In 1977 New York City had declared financial bankruptcy, and many industrial investors had then fled to more financially healthy cities. When I arrived in New York, its urban decay was impressive: wide swaths of the city looked like abandoned cemeteries, full of deserted factories and empty stores. But a visionary major named Ed Koch had a brilliant idea: he opened the city to artists and adventurous young people, inviting them to give new life to downtown neighborhoods, particularly to the East Village and the Lower East Side. Special grants and low rents were offered for urban renovation. Thousands flocked to the city and reinhabited lofts, turning them into places of creation, technical and existential experimentation, and cultural exchange. Musicians, artists, and techies made the city a sort of laboratory of possible futures. Visual art and music, and every kind of dope and erotic pleasure, pervaded these neighborhoods day and night.

Then AIDS came. AIDS made pleasure dangerous and jeopardized self-perception, dissolving the community of erotic, egalitarian friendship that had been flourishing worldwide for the last twenty years. The transition from conjunctive forms of communication to the digital purity of connectivity was inaugurated by the spread of this retrovirus. As the epidemic engendered fear of physical contact and dissolved the very possibility of imagining happiness, social energies migrated from the space of bodily conspiration (breathing together) to the space of disembodied communication.

I don't mean to suggest that the overall cultural involution that marked the eighties and paved the way to privatization and precarity can be reduced to the AIDS crisis, but the crisis's identification of pleasure with disease did slowly turn social life into a desert. Decades of social solidarity and free love came to an end, and the digital mutation followed, replacing conjunction with connection when digital technology pervaded the sphere of human communication. Even if it was transmitted by sexual contact, AIDS was mainly a psycho-media epidemic. It was based on the communication of a retrovirus, but it resulted in the communication of fear. When contact with the Other's body came to be perceived as a danger—and when this sense of danger took root in the social unconscious—language transmigrated from the conjunctive to the connective sphere. At that point, sadness settled in the social soul.

Depression may be described as the condition in which, no longer investing desire in daily experience, the conscious organism loses the ability to find meaning in its surrounding world. Actually, meaning does not lie in things, or in the signs of language. It is generated by the endless shift from one interpretation to the next, from the uncertain and ambiguous exchange of gestures. Desire is the energy that enables this continuous activity of interpretation. Meaning is the effect of affective communication among language agents. Since meaning emerges in the dimension of affective conjunction, the possibility of meaningful exchange rapidly dissolves when the community of bodies disaggregates. This is the starting point of depression.

Purity and Depression: The White American Soul

Purity (2015) is not Jonathan Franzen's best novel, in my opinion. However, this book may be the key to fully understanding the author's universe. *Purity* sheds new light on Franzen's previous books, revealing the general design of his colossal work, which is dedicated to outlining the decay of the American soul and the melting of the American brain. The novel offers clues to analyzing the white American sensibility, the resurfacing racist psychosis, and the ensuing escape toward the sphere of digital abstraction. *Purity* illuminates the obsession that lies behind the depressive mindscape of Franzen's two previous novels, *The Corrections* (2001) and *Freedom* (2010).

Purity is a novel about the Protestant obsession with truth, moral integrity, and perceptual clarity. Sweeping away the dust of indeterminacy, removing imprecision, denying the plurality of possibilities: these are the conditions for entering the sphere of digital formatting. The obsession with purity aims to erase ambiguousness, but it simultaneously removes the intimate awareness that nothing is pure in the living world, and that truth does not exist. In order to explain the universe of purity, Franzen speaks of the slow, painful embedding of the connective modality into the human mind and of the corollary neoliberal destruction of social solidarity and paralysis of sexual empathy for fear of contamination. As Franzen writes, "The aim of the Internet and its associated technologies was to 'liberate' humanity from the tasks—making things, learning things, remembering things—that had previously given meaning to life and thus had constituted life. Now it seemed as if the only task that meant anything was search-engine optimization. . . . if—and only if—you had enough money and/or tech capability, you could control your Internet persona and, thus, your destiny and your virtual afterlife. Optimize or die. Kill or be killed."[1]

Digital connectivity entails a continuous recombination of preformatted segments of nervous energy: the indeterminacy of social life is replaced by the code of determination, and in the end neoliberal individualism leads to automated fractalization. This is the sad "freedom" that Franzen speaks of in his earlier novel of that title. The digital self is obliged to get purified of its residual human empathy, compassion, and solidarity, in order to escape the downward spirals of misery and failure and tune in to the dynamics put in motion in the era of Margaret Thatcher and AIDS. When breathing together grew dangerous, everybody was obliged to breathe alone and the rhythm of individual respiration was obliged to follow the pace of economic competition.

Reading Franzen's work is the best way to gain insight into what is happening to the American mind, and particularly to the American unconscious, during the reign of Trump. Franzen's novels can be read as meticulous investigations of the molecular dynamics of contemporary depression—the subjective background of Trumpism. In Franzen's works, each a journey into the subcutaneous tunnels of the contemporary psycho-sphere, the depressive turn of contemporary Western culture is retraced and deciphered through the signs of language. In *Purity*, Franzen writes: "In his subatomic self, no chronology was stable."[2] The subatomic self has fractalized, losing the ability to conjoin with the Other. In a lonely dance in which friendship is forbidden, the inner self is obliged to instead synchronize with the pure abstraction of digital time. In *The Corrections* and in *Freedom*, Franzen outlines a phenomenology of American depression. *Purity* is less convincing, from a literary point of view, with its excess of philosophical consciousness and lack of compelling narrative. Nevertheless, this book is the best entrance into Franzen's fictive universe, and stands as a far-reaching essay on the genealogy, and also on the ontology, of American depression. This is a crucial point: we must understand that depression is not only a mental affliction, but may also be interpreted (and treated) as a way to approach truth, as a discourse about Being itself (as a discourse concerning the *ontos*, and therefore the truth).

The novel that first brought Franzen to my attention was *The Corrections*. This book, a metaphor for the rotting of the American brain, narrates the year-long preparation of Christmas dinner in the Lambert family. The three Lambert sons, all in their thirties, lead lives that oscillate between panic and depression. The father, a perfect example of the depressed and apathetic middle-class Midwesterner, is slowly descending into senility, and is more and more frail and dangerously unable to remember what he has done two minutes ago. The mother, at last, has just discovered the balm of psychopharmacology. While artificial intelligence is becoming the main area of research and innovation in Silicon Valley, the living brain of America is decaying, seized by anxiety and depression, furiously looking for scapegoats and for revenge.

One might say that Franzen is merely advancing the literary investigation that Don DeLillo commenced in the '80s—and this is partially true. But something new has happened between then and now. DeLillo is a contemporary of Jean Baudrillard's, and the dissolution of modern rationality and concomitant expansion of postmodern meaninglessness are described in his writings with a sort of breathlessly ironic excitement. Baudrillard and DeLillo similarly foretell social disintegration and the dissolution of social psychology. In DeLillo's writings, as in Baudrillard's, the unfolding of the apocalypse is seen from the point of view of a failed utopian imagination. But Franzen expresses the mood of the subsequent generation: for him, the loss of shared meaning is no longer a scandal or an affliction or an exciting adventure, but rather the permanent condition under which Western society (and not only it) has established itself. Thirty years after Baudrillard, Franzen recounts the postmodern theorist's dystopia as an insuperable norm, a loop that repeats without lines of escape.

In *Purity*, we discover that the adventure has happened long ago, in an age that can still be recalled but that cannot be revived. This adventure in the distant past left traces in the souls of the novel's characters who experienced it (Andreas Wolf, Abigail, Tom Abernat), but presently they live with a painful consciousness of falsehood, of inauthenticity. The novel's new generation of humans were born after the Event. (May '68? The exuberant countercultural movements? The hippy dream? The fall of the Berlin Wall in '89? The fertile nascency of the Internet in the '90s? Yes, all of this—and much more.) This generation has no memory of the special texture of human experience before and during the Event—experience in the dimension of impurity, of double meaning, of idle caressing and semio-erotic conjunction. The old world, experienceable before the digital reconfiguration, had a semiotics in which signs were allowed to carry more than one meaning, in which interpretation was both blurred and enriched by ambiguity. It was a world of hair: the long coiffure, the moustache, underarm hair, *los barbudos*, the black Afro, the untamed mane. In the digital sphere, hair is forbidden, haircutting is mandatory, and semiotic ambiguity is taboo. Any blurring indeterminacy or confusion would be inconsistent with the digital sphere's logic of connective machines and connective minds.

The mind of Pip Tyler (Purity Tyler, to be precise) is the central subject of *Purity*. Pip is a twenty-something perfectly proficient in the use of information technology and looking for a precarious job. She has a vague and uncertain sense of the fact that before her time an impure world once existed, but her distance from that world is total. The aesthetic, ethical, and cognitive configuration of her mind would not comply with the impure world of the past.

In DeLillo's works, the opening of an abyss of nothingness was breathtaking; in Franzen's, there is no more amazement because we are already installed in a long-lasting nothingness. In the digital mind, events do not exist; only info-neural stimuli register. If an event occurs, then we have to remove it from our consciousness as soon as possible. In *Freedom*, for example, the young Joey seems eager to erase the memory of what happened on September 11, 2001, for that event disturbs the expectations embedded in his mind: nothing has prepared him to internalize an event that disrupts the chain of predictability, that ruptures the smooth order of coded life. Joey experiences 9/11 as an unthinkable "glitch":

> Later, as his troubles began to mount, it would seem to him as if his very good luck, which his childhood had taught him to consider his birthright, had been trumped by a stroke of higher-order bad luck so wrong as not even to be real. He kept waiting for its wrongness, its fraudulence, to be exposed, and for the world to be set right again, so that he could have the college experience he'd expected. When this

failed to happen, he was gripped by an anger whose specific object refused to come into focus. The culprit, in hindsight, seemed *almost* like bin Laden, but not quite. The culprit was something deeper, something not political, something structurally malicious, like the bump in a sidewalk that trips you and lands you on your face when you're out innocently walking.[3]

Freedom without Friendship

The "freedom" that Franzen writes of is a freedom without friendship—that is, a freedom without meaning. The well-chiseled dialogues of his books are the bitter mirror of a humankind that has lost its ability to share the pleasure of existence. What offers us the possibility of finding meaning and pleasure in the occurrences of this life is a dialogic relation that establishes a space of mutual understanding. Meaning is interpersonal interpretation, a shared pathway of consciousness. Existence alone has no meaning: this is the truth that we learn from traversing the desert of meaninglessness. But this truth is not frightening so long as we can find oases in the desert: oases of friendship, love, intellectual and erotic sharing, conspiration and the projection of a common landscape. Such oases are the precondition for sensuous consciousness and for shared imagination.

Meaning is based on friendship, on dialogue among friends. Franzen's "freedom" lacks the warmth of friendship, and therefore lacks any perceivable meaning. The novel's main character, Patty, commits adultery in her search for meaning and for sharing. Her search fails, because in this world nobody is able to share joy and cynicism prevails over friendship. Patty, whose therapist has asked her to write an autobiography, can characterize her experience of time clinically: "Time passed in a peculiar manner which the autobiographer, with her now rather abundant experience of murdered afternoons, is able to identify as *depressive* (at once interminable and sickeningly swift; chock-full second-to-second, devoid of content hour-by-hour)."[4] *Freedom* is about female adultery, where betrayal registers the desire for freedom. As in *Madame Bovary*, here we also find the anguish of feminine freedom, but Flaubert's Emma suffered from a different kind of malaise—a boredom that resulted from a lack of stimuli, from the existential emptiness of the French provincial life of her time. Conversely, Patty suffers from a depressive anxiety that comes from an excess of stimuli, from an overload of promises, from an unlimited horizon of "opportunities" that will never translate to shared adventure or pleasure.

The personal biographies of writers are not always relevant, but Franzen's biography is interesting. His personal experience, recounted in his essay collection *Farther Away*, offers a revealing introduction to the eventless world his characters inhabit. Love, competition, and depression are intertwined in the story of his life as much as they are in his literary imagination. Here we can find the social background of his literary works. In an essay titled "On Autobiographical Fiction," Franzen recalls the end of his marriage:

> The first thing I had to do in the early nineties was get out of my marriage. Breaking the oath and the emotional bonds of loyalty is rarely an easy thing for anyone to do, and in my case it was particularly complicated by my having married another writer. I was dimly aware that we were too young and inexperienced to be making a lifetime vow of monogamy, but my literary ambition and my romantic idealism prevailed. We got married in the fall of 1982, when I had just turned twenty-three, and we set about working as a team to produce literary masterworks. Our plan was to work side by side all our lives. It didn't seem necessary to have a fallback plan, because my wife was a gifted and sophisticated New Yorker who seemed bound to succeed, probably long before I did, and I knew that I could always take care of myself. And so we both proceeded

to write novels, and we were both surprised and disappointed when my wife couldn't sell hers. When I did sell mine, in the fall of 1987, I felt simultaneously excited and very, very guilty. [. . .]

Fortunately, before my wife and I ended up killing ourselves or somebody else, reality intervened.[5]

Franzen's pitiless self-description here reveals the pathogenic relation between competition and love. He describes a truly American love, a love cold and cruel because it is based on a dangerous double bind: loyalty in competition, and competition in loyalty. A love that is quite protestant, puritanical, and white.

In this view, other living beings are essentially to be regarded as economic subjects, competitors. The epidemic of "I like" and the waterfall of "I love you" heard in daily conversation are the other side of an affective constipation and a fundamental social brutality. In the essay "Pain Won't Kill You" (a commencement address delivered at Kenyon College), Franzen touches on something similar: "Let me . . . point out how ubiquitously the word *sexy* is used to describe late-model gadgets; and how the extremely cool things that we can do now with these gadgets . . . would have looked, to people a hundred years ago, like a magician's incantations, a magician's hand gestures; and how, when we want to describe an erotic relationship that's working perfectly, we speak, indeed, of *magic*."[6] Franzen's point is that in America sentimentalism is linked to gadget aesthetics, and becomes a self-replicating virus of language. He continues: "A related phenomenon is the ongoing transformation, courtesy of Facebook, of the verb *to like* from a state of mind to an action that you perform with your computer mouse: from a feeling to an assertion of consumer choice. And liking, in general, is commercial culture's substitute for loving. The striking thing about all consumer products—and none more so than electronic devices and applications—is that they're designed to be immensely likable."[7] Franzen's America is the world that emerges from puritanical purification, from the erasure of the emotional memory of history. It is a world based on a fundamental lack of friendship, where solidarity has been replaced with verbal negotiation and convention.

Since its origin, the American community has been based on words: first, on the word of God; next, on the words of constitutional reason formulated in the Declaration of Independence, which inaugurated American identity as a tabula rasa. This purely verbal engine of American identity (well described by Samuel Huntington in *Who Are*

We?) is an anthropological and epistemological condition that has finally evolved into its perfect form—the digital.[8] Here the neohuman emerges, as the connective mutation cancels the ability to feel the conjunctive warmth of others, to receive the Other as a surprise that cannot be reduced to sentimentalism. In *Freedom*, Franzen observes that "the American experiment of self-government [was] statistically skewed from the outset, because it wasn't the people with sociable genes who fled the crowded Old World for the new continent; it was the people who didn't get along well with others."[9] These words remind me of the novels of Cormac McCarthy, a writer who describes in a less sophisticated but more direct way the sordid violence that can flourish in the antiaffective and brutal desert that is the anthropological ground of white American society. Franzen goes further than McCarthy does, because he shows the link between soulless brutality and digital culture. The digital mutation comes as the climax of a story that began with the most perfect genocide in human history—the elimination of the indigenous people living on the North American continent, and their replacement by the pure annihilating word of God—and that ended with a biotically desolate landscape.

Neohuman culture, the culture after the American experiment has been exported worldwide, is based on a denial and obliteration of the singular psychogenesis of consciousness. Consciousness can be uniformed and replaced by connective procedures, but the unconscious cannot be obliterated. The puritanical cancellation of history and lived memory does not remove the memory of the violence inflicted on America's indigenous population, nor on its millions of imported black slaves, nor on its physical environment and that of the planet itself. So America's brutalized unconscious explodes with no rational or political mediation.

In another essay, Franzen recalls seeing the digital mutation unfold in daily gestures:

> There was unfolding, after all, in New York in the late nineties, a seamless citywide transition from nicotine culture to cellular culture. One day the lump in the shirt pocket was Marlboros, the next day it was Motorola. One day the vulnerably unaccompanied pretty girl was occupying her hands and mouth and attention with a cigarette, the next day she was occupying them with a very important conversation with a person who wasn't you . . . Back in 1998, not long after I'd quit cigarettes, I would sit on the subway and watch other riders nervously folding and unfolding phones, or nibbling on the teatlike antennae

that all the phones then had, or just quietly
clutching their devices like a mother's hand, and
I would feel something close to sorry for them.[10]

Franzen relates that his friend Elisabeth thinks that
the epidemic of "I love you" permeating daily
discourse is not so bad: it strikes her as a healthy
reaction to the fundamental Protestantism of white
American culture. I pay my respect to Elisabeth
but I think that nothing could be said more super-
ficial. The epidemic of *I love you* is the most
extreme albeit most innocuous manifestation of
the basic deficit of emotional understanding, a sort
of imitation of affect, a uniformed counterfeiting
of the tenderness that once upon a time was a fea-
ture of the human nature, before America emerged
to extinguish it.

Purity describes the painful process of the con-
nective reformatting of the mind that has enabled
the neoliberal disintegration of social solidarity.
When social beings are identified as competitors,
when sexual empathy is replaced by fear of con-
tamination, then the connective mutation can
be accomplished. Cynical purity and intimate
frigidity are psychological features that explain and
define the digital age. The digital mutation is so
pervasive because it is not based on ideology or
politics. It is not a choice but an automatism; it
does not refer to laws or moral principles, but to

the neurophysical constitution of language and being. In *Purity*, Franzen writes: "You could cooperate with the system or you could oppose it, but the one thing you could never do, whether you were enjoying a secure and pleasant life or sitting in a prison, was not be in relation to it. If you substituted *networks* for *socialism*, you got the Internet."[11]

Neoliberal discourse is charged with a rhetoric of the individual, but neoliberal practice actually destroys individual freedom. Competition and conformism are two faces of the same coin in the sphere of the market. Individuals today no longer pursue autonomous life projects. Instead, they are fragments of precarious time, ceaselessly recombined fractals, connective units that must perfectly interface if they want to be effective under the rule of economic rentability. In the long run, the cult of individualism has revealed its false nature: What is the meaning of individuality if the only evaluative criterion of individual success is conformity to competition?

Indeterminacy is slowly replaced by the determination of code, and the digital self must be purified of its residual traces of human empathy, compassion, and solidarity in order to escape the whirlpools of failure. But the failure of individual narcissism is a given.

Quagmire

In *Freedom*, Franzen writes: "People came to this country for either money or freedom. If you don't have money, you cling to your freedoms all the more angrily. Even if smoking kills you, even if you can't afford to feed your kids, even if your kids are getting shot down by maniacs with assault rifles. You may be poor, but the one thing nobody can take away from you is the freedom to fuck up your life whatever way you want to. That's what Bill Clinton figured out—that we can't win elections by running against personal liberties. Especially not against guns, actually."[12]

The United States of America is often viewed as the source of the reinvigorating energy of technology, as a country that is able to rectify injustice with the force of democracy. At first, Obama's victory confirmed this illusion. But America's first black president woke the beast: the country's white unconscious rebelled against his incomprehensible success, and now this beast is devouring not only the phony American dream, but also the possibility of civil peace. The reinvigorating energy of technology might be siphoned in the nihilist whirlwind of the West, in the suicidal depression that results from white decline and from the inability to cope with it. The dark American soul that Cormac McCarthy describes in his books has been freaking out since 9/11: during the self-defeating wars of George Bush, during the financial collapse and recession of 2008, and during the wave of racist police violence on the eve of the Trump's ascent.

War is visible in the background of *Freedom*, but it is a distant war: the systematic devastation of Iraq and other catastrophic effects of the war there that Cheney promised would be a cakewalk are just a faraway echo. "Meanwhile the country was at war," Franzen writes, "but it was an odd sort of war in which, within a rounding error, the only casualties were on the other side."[13] Many Americans (indeed, a majority) rejoiced over the devastation of Iraq and of millions of innocent lives, because the war was an oblique punishment for the humiliation of 9/11. Many pointed out that Saddam Hussein had nothing to do with Al-Qaeda, but this sort of subtlety did not matter to people like Cheney and Bush. Halliburton and Blackwater and similar necro-enterprises were the only winners of this war. The privatization of war turned out to be the pinnacle of the neoliberal reformation, the beginning of the end of Western civilization that is now fully visible in the age of Trump.

In *Freedom* Franzen speaks of war speculators who have no understanding of the meaning of the Iraq War nor of the concrete conditions in which it is deploying: "The nation was fighting ugly ground wars in two countries, the planet was heating up like a toaster oven, and here at the 9:30 [Club], all around him, were hundreds of kids in the mould of the banana-bread-baking Sarah, with their sweet yearnings, their innocent entitlement—to what? To emotion. To unadulterated worship of a superspecial band. To being left to themselves to ritually repudiate, for an hour or two on a Saturday night, the cynicism and anger of their elders."[14] Ignorance and cynicism are closely intertwined, and the average white American mind is a permanent theater of both. *Freedom*'s Joey seems to epitomize the new generation of American entrepreneurs:

> Joey was glad to see that the taking of Iraq was every bit the cakewalk he'd expected it to be . . . He had not the foggiest notion of what a Basra storefront looked like; he suspected, for example, that plate-glass Breadmasters-style refrigerated pastry display windows might not fare well in a city of car bombings and 130-degree summer heat. But the bullshit of modern commerce was a language he'd been happy to find himself fluent in, and Kenny assured him that all that mattered was the appearance of tremendous activity and instantaneous results. "Make it look good *yesterday*," Kenny said, "and then we'll do our best here on the ground to catch up with how it looks. Jerry wants free markets overnight, and that's what we gotta give him." ("Jerry" was

Paul Bremer, head honcho in Baghdad, whom Kenny may or may not have even met.)[15]

Ignorance and cynicism intermingle in the aggressive landscape of the present, mainly (but not exclusively) in the US.

The meaning of the word "ignorance" must be examined here: "ignorance" refers to the sphere of what we don't know, either because it is impossible to know (so far) or because we are not curious or clever enough to know it. American ignorance, epitomized by the mind of "dotard" Trump, is of the second kind. The problem is now exacerbated by the fact that as the sphere of the knowable is expanding, the speed of information is accelerating and simultaneously the privatization of the education system and the assault of the media on human intelligence are lessening the critical ability of the social brain. So ignorance is growing at unprecedented levels.

But what is the meaning of the word "cynicism"? In his foreword to Peter Sloterdijk's *Critique of Cynical Reason*, Andreas Huyssen characterizes Sloterdijk's definition of the cynic as "a borderline melancholic able to channel the flow of depressive symptoms and to continue functioning in society despite constant nagging doubts about his pursuits."[16] Franzen's depiction of the cynic is equally interesting: Joey's cynical friend Jenna counsels him that "the world wasn't fair and was never going to be fair, that there would always be big winners and big losers, and that she personally, in the tragically finite life that she'd been given, preferred to be a winner and to surround herself with winners."[17] Jenna's notion of "winning" is at the core of cynicism. "Be a winner" is the fundamental injunction of white culture—where "winning" implies the removal of any moral judgment and morality is seen as a purely functional consideration of acting. In his *Critique*, Sloterdijk defines cynicism as "enlightened false consciousness— unhappy consciousness in modernized form. . . . a consciousness that, under the compulsions of self- preservation, continues to run itself, though run down, in a permanent moral self-denial. . . . It begins as plebeian 'individualism,' pantomimic, wily, and quick-witted."[18] The cynical person bends to the prevailing truth—which is not ethical truth—and in a certain sense we might say that cynicism is the surrender of Art to Nature, language giving up its creativity and surrendering to the automation of linguistic functionality. Irony, meanwhile, rises from the awareness that language is diverging from nature, and that the ethical principle does consist in respecting singularity.

Americans have chosen Donald Trump because he perfectly embodies that which is absolutely impenetrable by irony, absolutely inaccessible by culture, by humanity, by compassion. Trump's dumbness is an effect of the self-loathing that stems from the disconnect between America's mythology of infinite potency and its experienced reality of supreme impotence. The cynicism of Trumpism grows from the neoliberal Empire of Chaos; it is an aggressive self-assertion of losers who identify with a perceived winner, of humiliated people who identify with a humiliator in chief.

Postfactual Truth and Ethical Choice

There is a relation between purity and truth, and the special preference of the American public for politicians who lie is (or used to be?) well known.

President Clinton underwent an impeachment trial for lying about an intimate subject that had no connection to his political role. Lately, the subject of political truth has again taken central place, after the deluge of lies, fake news, and ludicrous manipulations that played a crucial role in Trump's campaign and first year in office. Thanks to the multiplication of shitstorms in the social networks and in the overall info-sphere, the regime of truth has been shaken, leading journalists and philosophers to wonder if we are dwelling in a postfactual discursive world.

In an article published by the online magazine *Granta*, Peter Pomerantsev writes, "By the time a fact-checker has caught a lie, thousands more have

been created, and the sheer volume of 'disinforma-
tion cascades' make unreality unstoppable. All that
matters is that the lie is clickable, and what deter-
mines that is how it feeds into people's existing
prejudices."[19] And he concludes: "When the Brexit
campaign announces 'Let's give our NHS the £350
million the EU takes every week' and, on winning
the referendum, the claim is shrugged off as a 'mis-
take' by one Brexit leader while another explains it
as 'an aspiration,' then it's clear we are living in a
'post-fact' or 'post-truth' world. Not merely a world
where politicians and media lie—they have always
lied—but one where they don't care whether they
tell the truth or not."[20] I'm not sure I agree with
this argument that the good old facts are dismissed
in the bad new sphere of post-truth discourse.

What do we mean when we say "reality" or
"fact"? Facts are made in the sphere of human con-
ventions; the term comes from the Latin *facere*,
meaning to make. A fact is the product of the fac-
tual semiosis of social individuals. And reality is the
psychodynamic point of intersection of countless
projections of simulation flows proceeding from
human organisms and from semiotic machines.
Reality does not preexist the act of semiosis and of
communication; rather, it is a construct emanating
from multiple subjectivities. Those who think that
the postmodern philosophers have destroyed the
foundations of ethical life and of democracy by

undermining faith in the factual truth are mistaking causes and effects: philosophers have not destroyed the theological ground of ethical life, they have simply announced that ethical life has no theological ground, that ethical life is a choice based on interpretation and existential sharing.

The logical sequence of cause and effect is scrambled, and the foundation of truth is forgotten. So ethical choice cannot be based on some theological certainty or some evident factual meaning. Ethical choice is based on a conflict of sensibilities, and on an ironic awareness of the relativity of our own world-simulation, of our projection of reality. The source of ethical awareness is not compliance with absolute theological or historical values, but empathic self-love that cannot be dissociated from the well-being of others.

Truth cannot be the ethical motivation of our choices, only solidarity can. The problem is that social solidarity has been jeopardized by the widespread precarization of labor and by the all-encompassing cult of competition. Thus political action is impotent and ineffective. Political action was once based on the possibility of choosing, deciding, and governing, but today choice is replaced by statistical prediction, decision by techno-linguistic automatisms, and government by automatic governance. The puritanical framework is broken, and baroque chaos has invaded the political scene.

CARNAGE

Lonely Daters

The expression "snowflake generation" refers to the psychological fragility of those who grew up in the digital anthropo-sphere: in colleges, students are now more likely to report that they have mental problems, that they are seriously distressed by ideas that run counter to their worldviews and by events and news that question the expectations artificially created by the advertising environment. Their self-reliance is shrinking as they overuse mental health services.

Summer 2016 marked a new step in the rush toward annihilation. A string of terrorist suicide acts in France and Germany, and fragmentary wars in the Middle East. A wave of migration from the Mediterranean Sea, and unrelenting rejection from European governments. Brexit, and the transformation of Turkey into a nationalist dictatorship with Islamist undertones. The soft coup in Brazil. Last, but not least, the breathtaking ascent of Trump on the American scene.

Then, all of a sudden, at the high point of this summer, newspapers and television stations focused on the launch of Pokémon GO. The hype around Pokémon GO may be viewed as an anticipation of the widespread creation of gated mental communities: enclosed spaces of simul-world sharing, a process of techno-withdrawal from the scene of history. Immersive technologies may be seen as tools for massive denial. A privileged audience avoids being mentally invaded by the catastrophes looming around the planet and creates a virtual environment of navigable experiences. The Pokémon GO player will get out of his nerd cubicle and will run after virtual insects or birds. As the real birds are disappearing and no real adventure can be pursued in the real countryside, Nintendo is providing a simulation of adventure and life.

In the disquieting Polanski film *Carnage*, Kate Winslett comments about her husband, an unpleasant lawyer who is ceaselessly checking and watching and touching his mobile phone, that for him what is distant is always more important than what is next to him. One could not better express the effect that the digital cellular convergence has produced in the urban landscape. Information is distant, a nerve stimulus that accelerates and intensifies up to the point of making what is near unreachable. A sort of reformatting of the social mind is underway, and this reformatting is not only investing the interactive space of semiotic exchange. It is running deeper, investing the sphere of cognition itself: perception, memory, language, orientation in space and time. The continuum of conjunctive experience is disrupted by the fractal simultaneity of connectivity. The emotional sphere is involved in this evolutionary process of cognitive automation: info-stimuli proliferate and the nervous system enters into a condition of permanent excitement and postponement.

According to surveys conducted by San Diego State University, Florida Atlantic University, and Widener University, those who were born between 1990 and 1994 have the lowest rate of sexual activity in the last hundred years. In *Sex by Numbers* (2015), David Spiegelhalter, a professor at Cambridge University, presents a survey which indicates that in the average world population, the frequency of sexual contact has decreased from five times per month in the '90s, to four times per month in the '00s, to three times per month in the current decade.[1] According to data reported by Pornhub, in 2015 four billion hours were spent watching porn movies, and the site received twenty-one billion visits. There is little time left after so many hours of media sex for real sex. Time for talking idly and caressing and foreplay is missing.

In the precarious dimension, time is mostly invested in the pursuit of salary, while recognition and nervous energy are permanently invested in social competition—so, little time can be spent in coupling, in slow eroticism, in pleasure. A postsexual culture and a postsexual aesthetics are taking shape among millennials worldwide. A young man named Ryan Hoover writes in a blog:

> I grew up with computers and the internet, shaping my world view and relationships. I'm considered a "digital native"
>
> Technology often brings us together but it has also spread generations apart. Try calling a millennial on the phone.
>
> Soon, future generations will be born into an AI world. Kids will form real, intimate relationships with artificial beings.
>
> And in many cases these replicants will be better than real people. They'll be smarter, kinder, more interesting.
>
> Will "AI natives" seek human relationships? Will they have sex?[2]

In this sharply ironic text, Hoover sees the two faces of the current evolution. The new generation of humans is having intimate relations with artificial beings, and tending to abandon the ambiguous, distressing, and sometimes brutal relations between people. Human sensibility is narrowing as humans are more and more immersed in an artificial context. As humans interact with automata, they forget their conjunctive finesse and their ability to detect signs of irony and of seduction. They replace vibrational sensibility with connective precision. Yes means yes, no means no. It is a vicious cycle. The more humans grow lonely and nervous, the more they will seek the company of less emotionally engaging androids; the more they seek the company of less emotionally engaging androids, the more humans will grow lonely and nervous. Sex is part of the universe of imprecision, of indetermination, a sphere that does not comply with connective perfection.

In June 2016, *Wired* magazine featured a survey about online dating. It reported that:

When sites like Match.com first came on the scene, way back in 1995, they gave singles a weird wide web of potential significant (and insignificant) others. You picked an age range, sure, and height requirements, fine, but your options expanded. Thanks to the all-inclusive power of the Internet, you were scrolling through goths and triathletes and electricians and investment bankers and chefs, and suddenly it didn't seem so crazy to start trading emails with someone who rooted for the wrong sports team or even lived across the country. These people didn't go to your college, and they didn't know your friends (or your mom). But 20 years later, that diverse pool of potential daters hasn't grown broader and deeper—it's been subdivided into stupidly specific zones.

As an example, the article described one dating site tailored to the socially elite:

> The League, for the uninitiated, is the ivy-covered country club of dating apps, designed for people who are "too popular as it is." There's a rigorous screening process—"We do all that dirty work for you"—that takes into account where your diplomas come from, the prestige of your titles, and, crucially, your influence on social media. Two months after the League's November 2014 launch, the wait list was 75,000 people long.
>
> This, let's be clear, is not a good thing—and not just because elitism is lame. Apps like the League go against the entire promise and thrill of online dating. [. . .]
>
> The League is just one of a gaggle of services that appeal to the better-heeled crowd; there's

also Sparkology, the Dating Lounge, and Luxy ("Tinder, minus the poor people"—no joke). The most selective of all, Raya, is invite-only— you basically have to be a celebrity with a sizable Instagram following to be asked. But specialization isn't just for snobs. Apps now exist for pairing people based on the right astrological sign (Align), an affinity for sci-fi (Trek Passions), similar eating habits (Veggiemate), and a love of weed (My420Mate). Having interests in common is not a bad thing—especially if, say, religious identity is important to you—but making sure every potential match has a beard (Bristlr) or is at least 6'4" (Tall People Meet) means interacting only with the segment of humanity we think we'll like. It's wrong and also ineffective, because the truth is, most of us are pretty terrible at knowing what, or who, we actually want.[3]

Rather than looking for the Other, online daters are often looking for a mirror. Narcissism meets rejection of the unfamiliar, of the unexpected.

In *Freedom*, Jonathan Franzen depicts the sexual imagery of the online generation as a mixture of hypersexualization with a lack of eroticism, of porn hyperstimulation with frigidity: "The kiddies were perennially enticing and perennially unsatisfying in much the same way that coke was unsatisfying:

whenever he was off it, he remembered it as fantastic and unbeatable and craved it, but as soon as he was on it again he remembered that it wasn't fantastic at all, it was sterile and empty: neuro-mechanistic, death-flavored. Nowadays especially, the young chicks were hyperactive in their screwing, hurrying through every position known to the species, doing this that and the other, their kiddie snatches too unfragrant and closely shaved to even register as human body parts."[4]

Death Is a Right

Among countless acts of violence and of self-annihilation in the summer of 2016, one was particularly distressing to me: at the end of that June, in the settlement of Kiryat Arba, a seventeen-year-old Palestinian boy named Muhammad Nasser Tarayrah stabbed a thirteen-year-old Jewish girl to death while she was sleeping in her bed, and was then killed himself by an Israeli soldier. The event was not surprising: Kiryat Arba is a place where Jewish families have illegally settled after evicting Palestinian families from their houses, and Tarayat had grown up in an environment of humiliation, misery, and impotent rage. Can we define his act as one of terrorism? No. It is, rather, an act of despair.

In the precarious intifada without political leadership that has randomly exploded around

Jerusalem, Palestinians of all ages commit acts that cannot be explained in military or political terms: they come out of their houses with knives and try to kill Israeli citizens, generally without success. Always, these knife-armed guerrillas achieve a different goal: they are killed by Israeli soldiers who are armed to the teeth. Is this an insurrection? I wouldn't say so. An insurrection is a collective action, a process that is grounded in long-lasting solidarity and generally hopes to subvert a regime. In the case of the knife intifada, we have only individual actors, lonely worriers whose weapons are clearly inept to accomplish any military goal. It is absolutely clear that these young Palestinians, stressed and anguished by the misery, humiliation, and systematic violence of the racist State of Israel, are killing themselves: suicide by cop. The young Tarayrah, in fact, before going to murder a child, had explained his gesture in a way that could not be clearer. He posted to his Facebook profile an appalling sentence: "Death is a right and I demand my right."[5]

Do we need anything more in order to understand the hidden meaning of the so-called terrorism that is tearing apart the very fabric of daily life in contemporary society? Suicide by terror is the only line of escape from the humiliation and hell of urban misery, from the hell of precariousness.

Fertility and the Ultimate War

Mussolini once wrote, "if cradles are empty, the nation becomes old and decays."[6]

Fascism was an aggressive manifestation of the potency of young people who felt marginalized by the bourgeoisie of the last century, while contemporary Trumpism is an expression of the despair of impotent old white people in the age of globalization. The expression "Trumpism" expresses much of the movement's impotent desire for supremacy: a supremacy that ignoramuses reclaim in the name of their own ignorance, a supremacy of those who are aggressively competitive but lack the intellectual means to achieve.

In the past century, Fascism was essentially a violent assault of young males excluded from economic and political power yet obliged to fight in national wars. In "The Futurist Manifesto," sexual potency and political aggression were linked in the fascist imagination. Fascism expressed a sense of actual belonging: its sense of community was based on mythologies of blood and nation, but the life of its communities was real and intense. Ignorance and inability to understand the universal meaning of humanism were the effects of a cult of particularity that was based on a true energy within a lived experience of belonging.

It is no longer so. Today, the features of the reactionary aggression embodied by Trumpism outline a different psycho-scape.

First of all, demographics have changed: the senescent white men of the Western world are plunging into a sort of mental mayhem based on impotence and self-loathing. People are voting for nationalist parties not because they feel the warm sentiment of belonging to a community, but because they long for that sentiment, which now belongs to the past. They grew up in an age of rampant individualism; they trusted the promises of neoliberal selfishness and then discovered they were losers; they trusted the neoliberal promise of individual success and they were deluded. Now it's too late to embrace a new hope, a new imagination: the only thing they can share is their hatred, their desire for revenge. Deceived expectations and frustrated individualism are not leading to the resurfacing of solidarity, but only to a desperate longing and a raging death wish.

A demographic decline is inscribed in the psychosexual evolution of the West, and the uneasiness of the social body is an effect of the hypercaloric food and the drugs that the white race is guzzling to soothe its anxiety. This demographic decline is also partially the result of sexual anorexia, and seems also to be provoked by a decrease in fertility. Recently, CNN reported on a study that found "plummeting" sperm counts in Western men:

Sperm counts of men in North America, Europe, Australia and New Zealand are plunging, according to a new analysis published Tuesday.

Among these men there has been a 52% decline in sperm concentration and a 59% decline in total sperm count over a nearly 40-year period ending in 2011, the analysis, published in the journal *Human Reproduction Update*, said.[7]

Talks about fertility have resurfaced recently in Europe, as the unconscious of the West is haunted by a fear of infiltration and genetic contamination. In secular France, women's fertility has been reinvigorated by public financing of procreation. In Catholic Poland, the ruling party grants a small sum of money to couples that give birth to fresh Polish babies. European nation-states are concerned by low birthrates and population decreases, and are investing resources in persuading people to procreate.

What is the source of the belief that procreating is better than not procreating? That is an enigma to me, but I think that this fixation cannot be understood unless we take into account the psychotic resurfacing of racism. Why should we be afraid of population decline? One might argue that a population decrease could generate an economic and fiscal problem, but if so the solution is at hand: we, the Europeans, should stimulate immigration and organize the reception and integration of more people from countries where misery and war are raging. This solution is the exact opposite of the paranoid rejection that Fortress Europe has opposed on the wave of migration coming from African, Middle Eastern, and Asian countries. In Italy, migrants are paying an important part of the country's social security income. We should therefore promote adoptions, facilitate procedures, give European citizenship to the hundreds of thousands of babies who are currently lost in Turkish or Libyan concentration camps. However, European political leaders and the majority of the European public univocally reject this solution. Why? The unspeakable answer is that the white race would be in danger of extinction. How awful.

The idiocy of protecting racial identity is mobilizing the energies of the ignorant worldwide, and ignorance is striving to reproduce itself.

Identity Is a Trap

The concept of identity is a ruse, based on a misunderstanding. Identity is the projection of some traits from the past on the imagination of the future. Identity does not exist, only identification exists. Identity is the fixation on a process of identification that generally reduces complexity to a predictable pattern of behavior, according to psychological needs or political intentions. Cultures exist in a perennial process of becoming and cultural evolution does not depend on ovaries or sperm or skin color—it depends on schools, on books, on friendships, on the sharing of resources and technology. Identity is based on an imaginary sense of belonging to a common past, while cultural becoming anticipates the futures inscribed in the present of social life.

Identity is a psycho-political construct that generally holds together a social body that has lost its sense of solidarity. Identity asserts itself through exclusion and aggression. When workers lose consciousness of their common interest, they start thinking of themselves as Serbs and Croats, as whites and blacks, as Muslims and Christians. Having lost the social war, they prepare for new wars on the basis of their belonging to imaginary identities. They need a father because they have lost their sense of fraternity. Fraternal singularity is the starting point for building social solidarity, a form of friendship that does not belong to and does not need identity because it is based on freedom and desire.

Only from disidentification can a nonoppressive community emerge. A nonauthoritarian society cannot be based on the community of being, but only on the community of becoming; not on the community of memory, but only on the community of experience; not on the territorial community, but only on the community of nomadic people who provisionally meet somewhere, then disperse and meet again if and when they wish.

An obsessive need for an imagined sense of belonging is the main link between the Fascism of the last century and the Trumpism of today, but this paradoxically is also the main difference between the two. In the twentieth century, the myth of identity (national, ethnic, religious) was based on the living experience of common life, but the reemergence of this myth in the twenty-first century has a different background: it is an effect of the defeat of internationalist culture, but it is no longer based on any real experience of commonality or territory.

WELCOME 2 HELL

Biorhythm and Algorithm

"Rhythm" means chaosmic singularization of time: rhythm scans time as the vibration of a singular breathing organism which is seeking to tune in to its surrounding chaos.

Although the theory elaborated by Wilhelm Fliess at the end of the nineteenth century about biorhythms is generally considered pseudoscientific, I appreciate the metaphorical potential of the concept of the biorhythm. Organisms are composed of vibrant matter, and the pulsations of an individual organism enter into a rhythmic relation with the pulsations of other surrounding individual organisms. This biorhythmic conjunction of conscious and sensitive organisms is a vibrating relation: through it, individual organisms seek a common rhythm, a common emotional ground of understanding, and this quest is a sort of oscillation that results in a possible (or impossible) syntony. Within the conjunctive sphere of the biorhythm, signification and interpretation are vibrational processes. When the process of signification is penetrated by connective machines, it undergoes a reformatting and mutates in a way that implies a reduction—a reduction to the syntactic logic of the algorithm.

The word "algorithm" comes from the name of the Arabic mathematician al-Khwarizmi—a name which literally means "from Khwarazm," and was originally Latinized as *Algorismus*—whose works introduced sophisticated mathematics to the West. Nevertheless, I prefer a different etymology and a different meaning. "Algorithm" for me has to do with the Greek word *algos*, meaning pain. Furthermore, the word "algid" refers to frigidity, both physical and emotional. So I suggest that the word "algorithm" has to do with frigidity and pain. Algorithmic pain results from the constriction of the organism, the stiffening of the vibrational agent of enunciation, and the reduction of the continuum of experience into the discreet logic of computation.

At present, as our social concatenation is being mediated by connective machines, human agency is undergoing a process of reformatting. In *Vibrant Matter*, Jane Bennet writes:

No one really knows what human agency is, or what humans are doing when they are said to perform as agents. In the face of every analysis, human agency remains something of a mystery. If we do not know just how it is that human agency operates, how can we be so sure that the processes through which nonhumans make their mark are qualitatively different?

An assemblage owes its agentic capacity to the vitality of the materialities that constitute it. Something like this congregational agency is called *shi* in the Chinese tradition. . . . *Shi* is the style, energy, propensity, trajectory, or élan inherent to a specific arrangement of things. Originally a word used in military strategy, *shi* emerged in the description of a good general who must be able to read and then ride the *shi* of a configuration of moods, winds, historical trends, and armaments: *shi* names the dynamic force emanating from a spatio-temporal configuration rather than from any particular element within it.

Again, the *shi* of an assemblage is vibratory.[1]

When the algorithm enters the realm of social concatenation, human modes of interaction are reformatted and algorithmic logic seizes vibrant concatenation, blocking biorhythmic oscillation and reducing the infinite range of variations to the binary of 0 and 1.

The insertion of the algorithm into the semiotic process interrupts the continuum of semiosis and life: the algorithm, a nonliving (nonvibrational) semiotic unit, breaks the living continuity of signification. In the connective domain, interpretation is reduced to syntactical recognition of discrete states. The vibrational sign is stiffened in order to be transcribed in the language of syntactic exactitude based on the logic of digital discontinuity. The ability to decode and to interpret ambiguousness and irony is lost in this transcription. Difference is interpreted according to the rules of repetition, and the edge of indeterminacy that makes possible poetical misunderstanding (or hyperunderstanding, or surplus understanding) is dulled, cancelled.

As the semio-sphere is reformatted according to the algorithm, the vibratory nature of the biorhythm is suffocated. Breathing is disturbed and poetry is frozen—poetry, the error that leads to the discovery of new continents of meaning, the excess that contains new imaginations and new possibilities.

Intelligence and Consciousness

In *Homo Deus*, Yuval Harari observes: "Until today, high intelligence always went hand in hand with a developed consciousness. Only conscious beings could perform tasks that required a lot of intelligence, such as playing chess, driving cars, diagnosing diseases or identifying terrorists. However, we are now developing new types of non-conscious intelligence that can perform such tasks far better than humans. For all these tasks are based on pattern recognition, and non-conscious algorithms may soon excel human intelligence in recognising patterns."[2] The distinction between intelligence and consciousness is the interesting point here. Intelligence is the faculty of recognizing patterns and of choosing between decidable alternatives. Deciding between decidable alternatives is a task that can be formalized and therefore performed by an algorithm. Consciousness, if I may reduce the complexity of this concept to a simple and insufficient definition, is the ability to decide between undecidable alternatives.

One might argue that the refinement and miniaturization of the intelligent machine, linked to the introduction of fuzzy dynamics in the quantic activity of AI, will lead androids to behave consciously, but this reasoning is not sound. It is philosophically false, because consciousness is not behavior, but self-perception and self-judgment, self-enjoyment and self-loathing. This is the distinctive feature—ethical and ultimately aesthetic— of what is called "consciousness." It is logically impossible to simulate such self-perception, because this would presuppose the existence of a self prior to the act of programming the intelligent machine. Harari continues his reflection: "As long as [intelligence and consciousness] went hand in hand, debating their relative value was just a pastime for philosophers. But in the twenty-first century, this is becoming an urgent political and economic issue. And it is sobering to realise that, at least for armies and corporations, the answer is straightforward: intelligence is mandatory but consciousness is optional."[3]

Enlightenment in Question, Again

In *Dialectic of Enlightenment*, a rhapsodic and fragmentary book written in 1942, Horkheimer and Adorno explain why "humanity, instead of entering a truly human state, is sinking into a new kind of barbarism":

> The increase in economic productivity which creates the conditions for a more just world also affords the technical apparatus and the social groups controlling it a disproportionate advantage over the rest of the population. The individual is entirely nullified in face of the economic powers. These powers are taking society's domination over nature to unimagined

heights. While individuals as such are vanishing before the apparatus they serve, they are provided for by that apparatus and better than ever before. In the unjust state of society the powerlessness and pliability of the masses increase with the quantity of goods allocated to them.[4]

Horkheimer and Adorno have clearly stated that the Enlightenment carries within itself the seed of its own destruction: the separation of reason from the social body, which operation is the core of Kantian rationalism and of the cults of abstraction and the law. Through Enlightenment values, universal reason is separated from the living body.

Romanticism arrived to reclaim the organic character of spiritual life, as a reaction against the separation of reason from history and from living time: the Romantics reclaimed the space and the time of cultural events, and asserted that thought could not be dissociated from the spiritual process of life, which has a temporality and a location. Nationalism emerged from the Romantics' reassertion of belonging, and at last identity politics replaced thought, as Alain Finkielkraut remarks in his book *The Defeat of the Mind*.[5] The Romantic cult of national identity was a reaction to the universality of reason, an attempt to find a territorial foundation for the deterritorialized universal principles of rationality.

The dialectic of belonging and universality runs through the history of late modernity—until globalization has now translated the universality of reason into the uniformity of economic law. The false universality of capital accumulation comes to reduce the diversity of cultural life to the rule of financial valorization, while cancelling the political sovereignty of nation-states. At this point a global reactionary movement erupts, based on the reclamation of national sovereignty and cultural identity. Identity (national and otherwise) reemerges at this juncture, after the impotent rebellion of many populations against the global submission of reason to the market. But this identitarian reaction is based on a double delusion. First of all, cultural identity is a construct based on the baroque combination of decaying global traits. Secondly, national sovereignty cannot be restored without breaking the integration of economic exchange and entering a global state of war. Indeed, this is what is actually happening now: war is breaking out everywhere, and slowly the map of the world is turning into a web of intractable conflicts.

The global market is the only universal value left in the wake of the neoliberal deregulation that led to the destruction of any rule or moral principle. But the universality of the market is not smoothly homogenizing humanity, but instead crushing our living differences and strangling the majority of us. In the last decade, many attempts were made to emancipate humans from the dictatorship of the market, but a way out from financial-digital domination could not be found. So reasserting the deceptive ghost of identity seems to be the only way to subvert the universal value of the market, or at least to escape its grip.

Let's go back to Horkheimer and Adorno's *Dialectic*: "If enlightenment does not assimilate reflection on this regressive moment, it seals its own fate. By leaving consideration of the destructive side of progress to its enemies, thought in its headlong rush into pragmatism is forfeiting its sublating character, and therefore its relation to truth. In the mysterious willingness of the technologically educated masses to fall under the spell of any despotism, in its self-destructive affinity to nationalist paranoia, in all this uncomprehended senselessness the weakness of contemporary theoretical understanding is evident."[6] In the Trump era, the self-destructiveness of the Enlightenment denounced by Adorno and Horkheimer is reaching its peak: the enlightening forces of science and technology have once again revealed their duplicity, and are finally devouring democracy and humanist self-determination.

The digital enlightenment, married to the forces of corporate finance, has so deeply damaged the living organism's sensibility that the organism is regressing to brutality. The light of abstraction perfectly illuminates the screens of the automaton, but all around us darkness is setting in. The Dark Enlightenment is intellectual awareness of the darkness that is now falling all around us, as an effect of the dazzling expansion of light. As James Bridle has recently observed in *New Dark Age*, "we find ourselves today connected to vast repositories of knowledge, and yet we have not learned to think. In fact, the opposite is true: that which was intended to enlighten the world in practice darkens it."[7]

Socialisme ou Barbarie

I want to consider the moral implications of the concept of the anthropocene. Under the dispassionate screen of science, this concept unveils our awareness that it is too late.

Originally, the term "anthropocene" was meant to denote our own geological epoch. From the geological point of view, the impact of man on the planet's environment is now deemed irreversible. The accumulation of greenhouse gas emissions has irreversibly altered the chemical composition of the earth's atmosphere and consequently its living environment. But the concept of the anthropocene, which goes well beyond geology, outlines a methodology based on irreversibility.

As we know, the word "irreversible" is incompatible with political art. The effects of political will and political action are supposed to be reversible by definition: an act of language can cancel a previous act of language and subvert its effects; an act of decision can cancel a previous act of decision. But when it comes to the chemical composition of the atmosphere—and, by the way, when it comes to the psycho-chemical composition of the social mind—the human will is impotent and subversion means nothing.

The exit from modern capitalism cannot be less than a tragedy, because the knots tied by colonial violence cannot be loosed without traumas. This has been known since 1914, when imperialist tensions unchained a world war among competing nationalisms, and paved the way for violent social revolutions. But the extent of the tragedy was not predictable one hundred years ago, and is not fully predictable now. One hundred years ago, capitalism and modernity were distinct notions, such that an exit from capitalism was conceivable inside the anthropological framework of modernity. Today, a political exit from capitalism seems to be out of the question, because in the new anthropological framework political decision has been replaced by automatic governance. At this point, the end of capitalism tends to be imaginable only as the end of civilization itself.

In the '80s of the last century, the words "post-modern" and "postcolonial" triumphantly entered the cultural lexicon, implying that a peaceful exit from the naughty forms of modernity was at hand. It was not, because the legacy of five hundred years of global exploitation and concentration of wealth consists in trends that seem to be irreversible: environmental devastation, impoverishment of social life, and systematic aggression against the psycho-sphere. The overuse of the prefix "post" since the 1980s ignored the tragic toll demanded by the mutation that came with the technological transformation of social production and communication.

Somebody said in 1968, "Socialisme ou barbarie." This was not a *jeu de mots*, it was a lucid prediction. That year was the peak of human progress, the peak of democracy as critical participation; since then we have been living through a continuous process of cultural devolution, political regression, and social impoverishment. Why? In '68, humankind reached the point of maximal convergence between technological knowledge and social consciousness. Since then, technological potency has steadily expanded while social consciousness has relatively decreased. As a result, technology now has an increasing power over social life, while society is no longer able to govern itself. At the historical juncture of '68, social consciousness was expected to take control of technological change and to direct it for the common good. But the opposite happened: the leftist parties and unions regarded technology as a danger rather than as an opportunity to be mastered and submitted to the social interest. Liberation from work was labeled "unemployment," and the Left engaged in countering the unstoppable technical transformation.

As democracy proved unable to govern the techno-anthropological change, the deregulation of finance and technology carried on dismantling preexisting forms of social consciousness. As an effect of neoliberal privatization, the educational system was subjugated to the need for profit, and critical thought was separated from research and development. At that point, the divarication between social consciousness and technological innovation widened and widened. We might conclude that, if the human experiment was aimed at expanding the sphere of rationality and reducing chaos, the human experiment is over. The very tools that enabled the expansion of rationality and human control (science, technology, industry, and information) have subsumed life to abstraction. And living warmth can only be found outside the icy walls of the citadel of reason.

Ethics in Apocalyptic Times

Civilization is not crumbling, it is only diverging from civility. Today, civility dissolves while civilization strengthens its uncivilized grip. The technological infrastructure that supports civilization is not going to collapse, but it is escaping the control of human reason and volition. On the other side of the coin, we are led to imagine that humans may survive only as long as they divorce themselves from humanity.

Modernity was all about the emancipation of man from the domination of nature: the law of the jungle was suspended by the rationality of the Leviathan. Now, the man-made machine seems to be turning into a second natural necessity: a hyper-Leviathan that is no longer under the control of human reason, but under the control of self-replicating and self-governing automatism. This is why political action seems impotent to change the course of social relations: the combination of corporate economy and digital technology has left the orbit of volition, and consequently human culture has abandoned the sphere of humanism that was defined by ontological freedom and by the effectiveness of political will. The project of modernity was aimed at suspending the law of nature, and politics was charged with expanding the space of social conventions. Social relations belong to the sphere of language, not nature, and linguistic conventions are not determined by natural law. This is why during modernity the law of the jungle was partially countered within the social sphere, and almost kept in abeyance. When capitalism went global, however, the economy subsumed technology by submitting knowledge to the rule of capital accumulation. From that point forward, the techno-economy acquired the potency and the inescapability of a second nature.

Quite paradoxically, the very forces that have enabled human independence from nature have morphed into a sort of artificial nature, as inflexible and pitiless as the law of the jungle once was. Interfaces of the computational machine now pervade every cell of social communication, and submit cognitive activity to an insensitive digital format. When the complexity of the man-made machine surpasses the abilities of the human mind to measure and to critically elaborate, we enter a domain of undecidability and immeasurability; modern humanism collapses. At the end of the '70s, when the neoliberal agenda was gaining ground, Darwinism met social philosophy and the law of the jungle was named "deregulation": a dismantling of the political castle in order to make way for the sociobiological struggle for survival. In the deregulated space of the economy, the conscious law of humans is cancelled, but this cancellation does not lead to freedom. Techno-linguistic automatisms replace the conscious will and rational legislation. The automaton is the ultimate effect of perfect deregulation: automated governance of the jungle.

Is there a way out from the jungle? This question needs to be reframed: Is there a possibility for ethical life in the age of the automated jungle? Some suggest that we should "not go gentle into that good night," that we should rebel and resist in the spirit of Dylan Thomas's refrain and "Rage, rage against the dying of the light."[8] I feel a sort of frustration with this rebellious attitude against humiliation and impotence. Humiliation is the energy that is fuelling Trumpism worldwide. Potency was the inmost character of the bourgeois culture of industrial progress, but potency has transmigrated from the social dimension to the technological structure, and the living organism has slowly been plunging into impotence. As the white dominators of the world are made to feel impotent, they are humiliated and rage against their own impotence, and vote for some arrogant dotard, who promises to make America (or Italy, or wherever) "great again."

When humiliation comes to strangle dignity and self-respect in the majority of people, we probably need the antidote that is called "humility"—even if this is a difficult lesson to learn, for someone who is not a believer. Humility is abhorrent to the modern mind. The spirit of conquest, the cults of innovation and enterprise reject humility, as do the revolutionary movements of the last two centuries which proclaimed the aggressive pride of self-assertion. Humility, meanwhile, has been preached by conservative zealots as a certain submission to the will of God that often means submission to human injustice. So what can "humility" mean for someone who does not believe in God and refuses to accept human injustice? Quite simply, "humility" can mean an acknowledgment of the intrinsic limits of human potency, and also an awareness of the impermanence of our acts, of our bodies, and of our very consciousnesses. Humility can be seen as the way to deal with the exhaustion of modern potency, which was always essentially the illusion of governing chaos.

Modern rationalism never actually subdued chaos; moderns simply managed to postpone the explosion of chaos. Now that chaos is finally here, we should not forget what Deleuze and Guattari say about chaos and the brain in their final book.[9] If we want to deal with chaos, they suggest, we have to tune in to the rhythm of the cosmos; if we want to breathe (to conspire) within the chaotic rhythmic acceleration, we should consider chaos not only as a foe, but also, and primarily, as an ally.

Humility has something to do with compassion. Compassion, in fact, means sharing our common inability to submit chaos to will: sharing passion, sharing passivity. I think that somehow the ultimate ground of social autonomy does not lie in activism, but in passivism.

Like Melville's Bartleby, "I would prefer not to."[10] This passivity has something to do with what Christians call "Grace." Grace is a condition of coincidence, of harmony with the singular *atman* and the cosmic *prana*. When the rhythm of desire coincides with the rhythm of God's will, Christian wisdom speaks of "grace." In materialistic terms, I dare to say that grace is the condition of tuning in to singular becoming with the cosmic game.

When I had my first asthma crisis, I felt for some time on the brink of panic and hurried to ingest as much air as I could. Then my sister, who is wiser than me, told me, "You don't need to breathe that much; try to calm down and breathe slowly and unrapaciously." So I did, and I could breathe.

During the G20 summit in Hamburg in July 2017, a thousand artists performed a march of zombies, their faces and bodies painted gray and white. The following day in the streets of the city, thousands of young women and men marched behind a banner that read "Welcome 2 hell." In the past twenty years the global movement, from Seattle to Genova to Occupy, has tried to stop the hellification of the world. We have marched, we have chanted, we have said words and expressed concepts and proclaimed predictions that have been confirmed by every deployment of the global crisis. In return, many of us have been beaten, repressed, imprisoned, and killed. In the end, everybody is now in hell.

The most urgent question for the next generation is, how to be happy in this hell? How to create autonomous spaces of happy survival in this hell? The next question is, how can we save and transmit the message of equality and friendship, while the worst tempest in history unfurls?

EXPIRATION

the last breath

> And we, who have always thought
> of happiness as *rising*, would feel
> the emotion that almost overwhelms us
> whenever a happy thing *falls*.
> —Rainer Maria Rilke, "The Tenth Elegy"

The Automaton and the Brute

Since 9/11, we have been living in a time of apocalypse. That day a war started between the Western powers and fanatical jihadists. Osama bin Laden won his confrontation with George W. Bush. This is the unspeakable truth that we are obliged to acknowledge more than fifteen years after the beginning of the endless and suicidal War on Terror. Bin Laden is dead, sure, but from the heavenly place where he dwells, he smiles as he watches the agonies the world's most powerful country is immersed in as a consequence of his provocation, of the idiocy of the Bush-Cheney clan, and, most of all, of the invincible potency of chaos. Don't forget that those who wage war against chaos will be defeated, as chaos feeds on war.

In 2016 we entered a new phase, which may be defined as one of global civil war: terror has taken the upper hand in the large majority of the world's countries, and it is here to stay as the Western powers seem unable to understand that there is no question of military force when the fight is between cynicism and despair. Western domination has pushed the majority of the planet's people into a condition of utter despair, while the neoliberal market has simultaneously enabled a cynical diffusion of weapons of all kinds. A large number of people of the last generation, particularly in the Islamic world but not only there, are in such despair that they would prefer to die than to live. This is why they are unstoppable; this is why they are winning. On August 24, 2017, CNN reported a declaration by KCNA, North Korea's state-run news agency, that the "The US should not forget that their opponent is armed with nuclear weapons and ballistic missiles" and should "wake up from their old way of thinking that their land is safe and the [*sic*] death is an affair of others."[1]

The divide that is breaking apart the United Kingdom (leavers against remainers), the United States (liberals against supremacists), Spain (unionists against half of the Catalan population), and many other countries of the world is not a political divide, an opposition that could eventually be managed in a democratic context of ideological conflict. It is a cultural divide that is disintegrating the very foundations of society and leading toward forms of more or less deadly civil war. The unbridgeable divide may be viewed as an opposition between those who are culturally unable to come to terms with the processes of globalization and urban minorities who are culturally prepared to do so. This is not, essentially, an economic divide: not all those who refuse globalization have been disadvantaged by it, and, more importantly, not all those who resign to live inside the global horizon are profiting from it. Rather, this divide is essentially between the ability and inability to envision a new cosmopolitan dimension for the future. But the majority of the Western population is now rebelling against globalization and attempting to reclaim an impossible return to sovereignty. They will not get what they want because what they want is impossible, but their impotence will fuel more rage, more racism, and more aggressiveness.

Therefore I ask myself, can the apocalypse be averted, or mastered? As the concept of the anthropocene implies, it is already too late. "They have planted the wind and will harvest the whirlwind," the Bible says.[2] The trends of environmental devastation, military destruction, and social wreckage have now taken on an irreversible and self-feeding character; they tend to expand their effects, and they tend to eliminate possible countermeasures. Brutality is more and more dominating social relations, and the economic machine of production is ruled more and more by inescapable automatisms.

The Automaton and the Brute are the two separated forms of existence of our time: neuro-totalitarianism and global civil war are the forms of life looming on the horizon of the future.

Is There an Autopilot in Human Evolution?

According to an Oxfam report that was made public at the Davos conference in January 2018, in 2016 inequality peaked: 82 percent of the wealth produced that year was hijacked by the 1 percent of the world's population that already owns two-thirds of the world's wealth.[3] This is not a joke or an exaggeration: this is a documented proof of the demented nature of financial absolutism. Like a drain pump, financial capitalism has been sucking life from the organism of human society, at a rate that is accelerating by the second.

The question is, why are people doing this? Why is a small fraction of humankind accumulating an unimaginable amount of wealth, while the gross majority of humankind is regressing toward misery? What motivates this enormous appropriation of common resources? Indeed, is there a motivation, or does the logic of financial accumulation automatically produce this irrational and immoral effect? Lastly, what is the point of accumulating and hoarding uncountable billions that could never all be exchanged for goods or pleasure in this lifetime?

I don't think that greed sufficiently explains this extreme concentration of wealth in the hands of a precious few. Should we rather explain this irrational inequality in terms of an evolutionary survival instinct? Can I even speak of an evolutionary instinct of humankind, does such a thing exist? Probably not, but I'm trying to find a sort of autopilot in human evolution. The survival instinct is alert today, because we sense (even if we tend to deny the evidence and reject this knowledge in our collective unconscious) that civilized life on planet earth is approaching its end. Our collective unconscious senses that the final stampede is drawing nearer because of so many unstoppable and irreversible processes: proliferation of nuclear weapons, global warming, water scarcity, demographic expansion and desertification, and, last but not least, mental collapse, spreading depression and panic. It is totally understandable at this point for a human to be, whether consciously or not, preparing for a flight from planet hell. And preparing to escape from hell is inconceivably expensive. The 1 percent of humankind is preparing for this flight, and they need huge amounts of financial resources to do so.

Dystopian science fiction? Perhaps. Don't forget, however, that in the last fifty years dystopian science fiction has produced the most accurate roadmaps of our social and political becoming.

Now we understand what Günther Anders meant in *We, Sons of Eichmann* when he wrote: "we can expect that the horrors of the Reich to come will vastly eclipse the horrors of yesterday's Reich. Doubtless, when one day our children or grandchildren, proud of their perfect 'co-mechanization' look down from the great heights of their thousand year reich at yesterday's empire, at the so-called 'third' Reich, it will seem to them merely a minor, provincial experiment."[4] Hitler's Nazism, which in the second half of the last century we deemed defeated and nullified forever, was only an experiment in annihilation. That experiment failed, but the conditions are now set for its implementation. The swastika-tattooed Nazi hacker and troll known by his screen name "weev" wrote in an Alt-Right blog: "We need to put these people in the oven... We are headed for a Malthusian crisis. Plankton levels are dropping. Bees are dying. There are tortilla riots in Mexico, the highest wheat prices in 30-odd years... The question we have to answer is: How do we kill four of the world's six billion people in the most just way possible?"[5] I think that this is the semiserious, semiconscious subtext of the agenda forwarded under the banner of financial governance. Trump culture (forgive me the oxymoron) is the Dark Enlightenment that unveils the inmost dynamics of financial capitalism.

Ethical Apocalypse

Four decades of neoliberal reform have unleashed an ethical apocalypse: both empathy and universality, the two roots of ethical behavior, have been torn away. Empathy, the perception of the Other's body as an extension of one's own, is under increasing threat. Since neoliberal reformers have put competition at the core of daily life, and since digital connectivity has replaced physical conjunction in the sphere of social communication, the psychocultural conditions of empathy have been undermined. Likewise, the universality of ethical rule has been uprooted by the processes of globalization. Globalization is based on the primacy of economic competition, and effective competition demands the deletion of all rules—moral, political, or otherwise. This trend toward annihilation of ethical judgment seems to be self-feeding, and therefore irreversible; economic efficiency is based on disregarding the ethical implications of actions, and so ethical behavior becomes inefficient.

In a 1946 text titled *The Question of German Guilt*, Karl Jaspers distinguished between historical Nazism and quintessential Nazism.[6] Historical Nazism has been defeated, he says, but the cult of efficiency has not been, and this cult of efficiency is the core of quintessential Nazism. Economic competition does not accept any political regulation, any ethical limitation: cynicism, the systematic disregard for ethics, is a common feature of Nazism and the neoliberal cult of competition. The difference lies in the fact that Nazism was based on political violence and military dictatorship, while today's global competition is based on the embedding of technological automatisms into the living body of society.

This is why the rebels who marched against the G7 summit in Hamburg in July 2017 carried a banner welcoming everybody to hell. The question that we must answer now is, can we speak of ethical behavior in hell? The first answer that comes to my mind is no. No, because in hell empathy is self-harming. Empathic sensibility, in fact, is an open door to the inflow of surrounding suffering. This is why in hell people tend to keep to themselves and tend to close their empathic doors—in order to avoid being harmed by the spreading violence and surrounding suffering.

In her 1993 novel *Parable of the Sower*, Octavia Butler offers a dystopian premonition of a world filled with violence, starvation, and pain, where people are so accustomed to their surrounding hell that they are emotionally indifferent and dumb. In the book, a young girl suffers from a rare disease that her doctors call "organic delusional syndrome." This is how the character narrates her condition:

[My father] has always pretended, or perhaps believed, that my hyperempathy syndrome was something I could shake off and forget about. The sharing isn't real, after all. It's not some magic or ESP that allows me to share the pain or the pleasure of other people. It's delusional. [. . .]

I can't do a thing about my hyperempathy, no matter what Dad thinks or wants or wishes. I feel what I see others feeling or what I believe they feel. Hyperempathy is what the doctors call an "organic delusional syndrome." Big shit. It hurts, that's all I know. Thanks to Paracetco, the small pill, the particular drug my mother chose to abuse before my birth killed her, I'm crazy. I get a lot of grief that doesn't belong to me, and that isn't real. But it hurts.

I'm supposed to share pleasure *and* pain, but there isn't much pleasure around these days.[7]

Empathy is actually a liability and an economic disadvantage in the society of all-encompassing competition. The suffering of others is irrelevant from the point of view of the economic actor, who knows very well that *mors tua vita mea* (your death, my life). And the pleasure of others is likewise irrelevant, for it is either undetectable, nonexistent, or confused with advertising's artificial displays of joy.

Since this book is about breathing as a vibrational search to attune oneself to one's environment, I must say at this point that in the social sphere (the sphere of conspiration) this search is currently destined to fail. People feel this impossibility and they tend to become selfish and cynical, and therefore depressed and self-loathing. Since solidarity has been cancelled, only revenge is left: revenge of the impoverished against the oppressed (racism), revenge of the oppressed against women (macho violence), revenge of everybody against everybody else (brutality).

So I'm trying to displace the field of the vibrational search from social conspiration to cosmic expiration, to the dissolution of the individual (me) into the cosmic dimension of nothingness. What is the rhythm of nothingness? Orgasmic vibration is an example of attuning with the bio-rhythms of another body: sinking into unconsciousness may suddenly fling wide the doors of cosmic perception. The French call orgasm *petite mort* (little death), meaning an intense momentary loss or weakening of consciousness that enables a vision of nothingness and simultaneously opens the possibility of listening to the sound of chaosmosis.

Philosophy must consciously forge concepts for the attunement of the mind and body to the process of becoming nothingness. Poetry has to prepare our lungs to breathe at the rhythm of death.

The Last Breath of Lazarus

Death has been an object of psychological denial in the enlightened sphere of modernity. The cult of power that energized capitalist development marginalized and cancelled the consciousness of our mortality, our impermanence. In *Symbolic Exchange and Death*, Jean Baudrillard reflects on death as a subversive line of escape. An ironic perception of death is urgently needed, and poetry is currently working on it.[8]

In his last album, *Blackstar*, which is a meditation on death, David Bowie dared to look ironically at his own extinction. Old, sick, and beautiful, with a bandage over his eyes, his music video for the album's title track shows us a small book with a black star on its cover and announces to us, the survivors, that death is the horizon of life. Dressed as a snake, Lazarus rises from the grave and dances and remembers the days when we in New York were all living like kings, in the '70s and the early '80s. "By the time I got to New York / I was living like a king," Bowie sings. Powders then promised eternal life. And eternal life we got. Moribund people are dancing on stage. The video for "Blackstar" is exhilarating, lugubrious, and heartbreaking: "On the day of execution, on the day of execution / Only women kneel and smile [. . .] Something happened on the day he died / Spirit rose a meter then stepped aside / Somebody else took his place, and bravely cried / (I'm a blackstar, I'm a star star, I'm a blackstar)." Bowie shows us the beauty of old age, when old age is consciously and happily projected toward the eternity of nothingness. In the album's song "Lazarus," he sings: "Look up here, I'm in heaven / I've got scars that can't be seen / I've got drama, can't be stolen / Everybody knows me now / Look up here, man, I'm in danger / I've got nothing left to lose / I'm so high, it makes my brain whirl / Dropped my cell phone down below."

From Silicon Valley comes the promise of eternal technological survival and in Brazil some surgeons promise to remove all Lazarus's wrinkles. But this flavorless promise of longevity smells fake. We are powder and the powders remind us that we are powder. No one before Bowie had dared to sing of death in this manner, laughing and dancing and crying, and walking backward into the sepulchral wardrobe and disappearing behind the closet door, then closing the door. Do you remember Major Tom stepping through the door of the starship and entering the infinite darkness? "This is Major Tom to Ground Control / I'm stepping through the door / And I'm floating in the most peculiar way / And the stars look very different today." Forty years later, someone finds him dead and transformed to stone.

All through his life David Bowie portrayed the mutant, the alien, the visitor. In Nicholas Roeg's 1976 movie *The Man Who Fell to Earth*, Bowie comes from a distant planet, where drought threatens total extinction, to live on the earth under the name of Newton. He has left his wife and his children on his distant home planet and promised to return to save them from the deadly drought. Although he is the bearer of advanced technological knowledge, he is defeated by the brutality of men. Newton can see the future, but the future has been torn, so he turns into Bowie and is stuck on planet earth, despairing and alone, with no way out.

Mysterium Coniunctionis

After billions of years of evolution, substances transmuted into words. After combining and recombining atoms for countless eons, at a certain (uncertain) point matter entered into the cycle of signification. Wars, love, excitement, and elegance followed, and sensitive organisms went walking hand in hand over the bridge that transcends the primordial abyss of the absence of meaning. So we named the millennia and we stayed at the top of the hill, gazing hopefully for a light in the distance.

Then everything dissolved as an effect of acceleration, and now human signs are turning back into their original magma, where light glitters for no eyes and information is eternally silent. Frail is the architecture of happiness and heavy is the architecture of depression, as everybody knows. We all know from experience that brightness is easily shadowed, while the ensuing darkness is not as easy to dispel.

Let's think of the oscillation between darkness and brightness in the history of social movements. Let's think of the sudden explosion of euphoria in urban insurrections, subversive cooperation, shared creation, squatting, and sustained occupation of buildings, streets, and squares. A social movement is essentially a shared illusion of sympathy among conscious and sensitive organisms who conjoin in a social process.

Society is an imaginary sphere in which different processes of signification interweave and interfere. The symbolic organization of this imaginary sphere is an effect of signification.

I define "signification" as the building of a bridge of shared illusions over the abyss of the absence of meaning. Reality, by contrast, can be described as the psychodynamic projection of countless mental flows that interweave and inter- sect, building castles of language that we call different names: civilization, history, revolution, community.

Unhappiness exists—this is easy to understand. It's more difficult to assert what happiness is, and if it actually exists anywhere. We can argue that happiness is a vague perception of the inner self's harmony with the ongoing flow of perception, and also that it is the sudden and random synchrony of a singular vibration with the cosmic game. Christians call this state "grace." We experience happiness as the conscious suspension of the sight of the abyss. In those moments of suspension, we can build something: bridges over the abyss itself.

Groundlessness, emptiness, and the decomposi- tion of the bodily self: these are the abyss that all human beings are experiencing. But women and men can happily walk over this abyss if they understand that friendship resides in the ability to share the illusion of meaning. When the illusion of meaning is shared, it is no longer an illusion: it becomes reality. The bridge over the abyss is the dialogue that allows for the sharing of a vision, of an expectation, of an intention. This dialogue is based on refrains of nonattachment, and it emancipates us from the fear of not being. Getting freed from the will to live is the condition for being alive at last. The bridge over the abyss of the absence of meaning can take many forms: falling in love, tenderness, collective creation, hallucination, and movement. These forms give birth to the physical experience of meaning.

Meaning is not a presence, but an experience. Meaning is an effect of signification that does not belong to nature, but only exists in consciousness: a floating composition of neurological flows, of bodily and psychological matter that takes a form. Friendship is the condition for the experience—the existence—of meaning.

Notes

Introduction

1. Franco Berardi, *The Uprising: On Poetry and Finance* (Los Angeles: Semiotext(e), 2012).

1. I Can't Breathe

1. Friedrich Hölderlin, "Mnemosyne," in *Hymns and Fragments*, trans. Richard Sieburth (Princeton, NJ: Princeton University Press, 1984), 117.

2. Friedrich Hölderlin, "Remembrance," in *Hymns and Fragments*, 109.

3. Friedrich Hölderlin, "In Lovely Blue," in *Hymns and Fragments*, 249.

4. Ibid.

5. Ibid., 251.

6. Sigmund Freud, "Das Innere Ausland," in *Traumdeutung*, (Franz Deuticke: Leipzig und Wien 1939), Chapter 7.

7. Hölderlin, "In Lovely Blue," 251.

8. See Félix Guattari, *Chaosmosis: An Ethico-Aesthetic Paradigm*, trans. Paul Bains and Julian Pefanis (Bloomington: Indiana University Press, 1995).

2. Voice Sound Noise

1. Félix Guattari, *Chaosmosis: An Ethico-Aesthetic Paradigm*, trans. Paul Bains and Julian Pefanis (Bloomington: Indiana University Press, 1995).

2. Ibid., 135.

3. Byung-Chul Han, *In the Swarm: Digital Prospects* (Cambridge, MA: MIT Press, 2017), 3–6.

4. Cited in Jacques Attali, *Noise: The Political Economy of Music*, trans. Brian Massumi (Manchester: Manchester University Press, 1985), 87.

5. See Steve Goodman, *Sonic Warfare: Sound, Affect, and the Ecology of Fear* (Cambridge, MA: MIT Press, 2010).

6. Robert J. Sordello, *Money and the Soul of the World* (TK: Pegasus Foundation, 1983), 1, 2.

7. Ludwig Wittgenstein, *Tractatus Logico-Philosophicus*, trans. D. F. Pears and B. F. McGuinness (London: Routledge, 2001), 3.

8. Ibid., 68–69.

9. Guattari, *Chaosmosis*, 85.

3. Chaos and the Baroque

1. See José Antonio Maravall, *Culture of the Baroque* (Manchester: Manchester University Press, 1986).

2. Cited in Chunglin Kwa, *Styles of Knowing: A New History of Science from Ancient Times to the Present*, trans. David McKay (Pittsburgh: University of Pittsburgh Press, 2011), 205.

4. Chaos and the Brain

Epigraph: Rainer Maria Rilke, "The Eighth Elegy," in *Duino Elegies and The Sonnets to Orpheus*, trans. Stephen Mitchell (New York: Vintage International, 2009), 51.

1. Antonio Spadaro, "A Big Heart Open to God: An Interview with Pope Francis," *America* vol. 209, no. 8 (30 September 2013), https://www.americamagazine.org/faith/2013/09/30/big-heart-open-god-interview-pope-francis.

2. Gilles Deleuze and Félix Guattari, *What Is Philosophy?*, trans. Hugh Tomlinson and Graham Burchell (New York: Columbia University Press, 1994), 201.

3. Ibid., 203.

4. Ibid.

5. Ludwig Wittgenstein, *Tractatus Logico-Philosophicus*, trans. D. F. Pears and B. F. McGuinness (London: Routledge, 2001), 68.

6. Deleuze and Guattari, *What Is Philosophy?*, 208.

7. Ibid., 201.

8. William Shakespeare, *Macbeth*, ed. Stephen Orgel (New York: Penguin Books, 2000), 92.

5. Chaos and Control

1. G. W. Leibniz, *Monadology*, in G. W. Leibniz's *Monadology: An Edition for Students*, ed. and trans. Nicholas Rescher (Pittsburgh: University of Pittsburgh Press, 1991), 87.

2. G. W. Leibniz, "Principles of Nature and Grace, Based on Reason," in *Philosophical Essays*, ed. and trans. Roger Ariew and Daniel Garber (Indianapolis: Hackett, 1989), 211.

3. Leibniz, *Monadology*, 221.

4. Ibid., 162.

5. Arjun Kharpal, "Elon Musk: Humans must merge with machines or become irrelevant in AI age," CNBC, 13 February 2017, https://www.cnbc.com/2017/02/13/elon-musk-humans-merge-machines-cyborg-artificial-intelligence-robots.html.

6. Purity

Epigraph: Jonathan Franzen, *Purity* (New York: Farrar, Straus and Giroux, 2015), 450.

1. Franzen, *Purity*, 492.

2. Ibid., 460.

3. Jonathan Franzen, *Freedom* (New York: Farrar, Straus and Giroux, 2010), 232 and 233.

4. Ibid., 114.

5. Jonathan Franzen, "On Autobiographical Fiction," in *Farther Away* (New York: Farrar, Straus and Giroux, 2012), 131–32.

6. Jonathan Franzen, "Pain Won't Kill You," in *Farther Away*, 6.

7. Ibid., 7.

8. Samuel Huntington, *Who Are We?: The Challenges to America's National Identity* (New York: Simon and Schuster, 2004).

9. Franzen, *Freedom*, 444.

10. Franzen, "I Just Called to Say I Love You," in *Farther Away*, 145.

11. Franzen, *Purity*, 448.

12. Franzen, *Freedom*, 361.

13. Ibid., 399.

14. Ibid., 369.

15. Ibid., 399–402.

16. Andreas Huyssen, "The Return of Diogenes as Postmodern Intellectual," foreword to *Critique of Cynical Reason*, by Peter

Sloterdijk, trans. Michael Eldred (Minneapolis: University of Minnesota Press, 1987), xii.

17. Franzen, *Freedom*, 402.

18. Sloterdijk, *Critique*, 217–18.

19. Peter Pomerantsev, "Why We're Post-Fact," *Granta*, 20 July 2016, https://granta.com/why-were-post-fact/.

20. Ibid.

7. Carnage

1. David Spiegelhalter, *Sex by Numbers: What Statistics Can Tell Us about Sexual Behavior* (London: Profile Books, 2015).

2. Ryan Hoover, "Artificial Intelligence Natives," *Medium*, 16 October 2016, https://medium.com/@rrhoover/artificial-intelligence-natives-10a9843aa9a1.

3. Elise Craig, "Niche Dating Apps Like the League Are Icky and Bad for Love," *Wired*, 7 June 2016, https://www.wired.com/2016/06/why-tinder-is-bad.

4. Jonathan Franzen, *Freedom* (New York: Farrar, Straus and Giroux, 2010), 348–49.

5. Cited in Don Lieber, "Kiryat Arba Killer Had a Death Wish, Facebook Posts Show," *Times of Israel*, 30 June 2016, https://www.timesofisrael.com/kiryat-arba-attacker-had-a-death-wish-facebook-posts-show.

6. Cited in Simonetta Falasca-Zamponi, *Fascist Spectacle: The Aesthetics of Power in Mussolini's Italy* (Berkeley: University of California Press, 2000), 257n45.

7. Susan Scutti, "Sperm Counts of Western Men Plummeting, Analysis Finds," *CNN*, 25 July 2017, https://edition.cnn.com/2017/07/25/health/sperm-counts-declining-study/index.html.

8. Welcome 2 Hell

1. Jane Bennett, *Vibrant Matter: A Political Ecology of Things* (Durham, NC: Duke University Press, 2010), 34–35.

2. Yuval Noah Harari, *Homo Deus: A Brief History of Tomorrow* (New York: HarperCollins, 2017), 314.

3. Ibid.

4. Max Horkheimer and Theodor W. Adorno, *Dialectic of Enlightenment: Philosophical Fragments*, ed. Guzelin Schmid Noerr, trans. Edmund Jephcott (Stanford, CA: Stanford University Press, 2002), xiv and xvii.

5. Alain Finkielkraut, *The Defeat of the Mind*, trans. Judith Friedlander (New York: Columbia University Press, 1995).

6. Horkheimer and Adorno, *Dialectic*, xvi.

7. James Bridle, *New Dark Age: Technology and the End of the Future* (London: Verso, 2018), 10.

8. Dylan Thomas, "Do not go gentle into that good night," in *The Poems of Dylan Thomas*, ed. John Goodby (New York: New Directions, 2017), 193.

9. Gilles Deleuze and Félix Guattari, *What Is Philosophy?*, trans. Hugh Tomlinson and Graham Burchell (New York: Columbia University Press, 1994).

10. See Herman Melville, "Bartleby, the Scrivener: A Story of Wall-Street," in *Great Short Works of Herman Melville*, ed. Warner Berthoff (New York: Perennial Classics, 2004), 39–74.

9. Expiration

Epigraph: Rainer Maria Rilke, "The Eighth Elegy," in *Duino Elegies and The Sonnets to Orpheus*, trans. Stephen Mitchell (New York: Vintage International, 2009), 67.

1. Zachary Cohen, "North Korea Mocks Trump's Twitter Habits, Condemns US Military Drills," CNN, 24 August 2017, https://www.cnn.com/2017/08/23/politics/north-korea-condemns-us-south-korea-drills/index.html.

2. Hosea 8:7 (New Living Translation).

3. Oxfam International, *Reward Work, Not Wealth*, January 2018, https://www.oxfam.org/en/research/reward-work-not-wealth.

4. Günther Anders, *We, Sons of Eichmann: An Open Letter to Klaus Eichmann*, trans. Jordan Levinson, http://anticoncept.phpnet.us/eichmann.htm.

5. Cited in Angela Nagle, *Kill All Normies: Online Culture Wars from 4Chan and Tumblr to Trump and the Alt-Right* (Alresford: Zero Books, 2017), 141.

6. Karl Jaspers, *The Question of German Guilt*, trans. E. B. Ashton (New York: Fordham University Press, 2000).

7. Octavia Buter, *Parable of the Sower* (New York: Grand Central, 2000), 11–12.

8. Jean Baudrillard, *Symbolic Exchange and Death*, trans. Iain Hamilton Grant (London: SAGE, 1993).

ABOUT THE AUTHOR

Franco Berardi, aka "Bifo," founder of the famous "Radio Alice" in Bologna and an important figure of the Italian Autonomia Movement, is a writer, media theorist, and media activist. He currently teaches Social History of the Media at the Accademia di Brera, Milan.